WRITE YOUR WAY IN

The Craft of Research
Wayne C. Booth, Gregory G. Colomb, Joseph M. Williams, Joseph Bizup, and William T. FitzGerald

The Chicago Guide to Grammar, Usage, and Punctuation
Bryan A. Garner

The Art of Creative Research
Philip Gerard

From Dissertation to Book
William Germano

Getting It Published
William Germano

Storycraft
Jack Hart

A Poet's Guide to Poetry
Mary Kinzie

How to Write a BA Thesis
Charles Lipson

The Subversive Copy Editor
Carol Fisher Saller

The Writer's Diet
Helen Sword

A Manual for Writers of Research Papers, Theses, and Dissertations
Kate L. Turabian

Student's Guide to Writing College Papers
Kate L. Turabian

Write Your Way In

CRAFTING AN UNFORGETTABLE COLLEGE ADMISSIONS ESSAY

Rachel Toor

The University of Chicago Press
Chicago and London

The University of Chicago Press, Chicago 60637
The University of Chicago Press, Ltd., London

Published 2017.
Printed in the United States of America

26 25 24 23 22 21 20 19 18 17   2 3 4 5

ISBN-13: 978-0-226-38375-0 (cloth)
ISBN-13: 978-0-226-38389-7 (paper)
ISBN-13: 978-0-226-38392-7 (e-book)
DOI: 10.7208/chicago/9780226383927.001.0001

Library of Congress Cataloging-in-Publication Data
Names: Toor, Rachel, author.
Title: Write your way in : crafting an unforgettable college admissions essay / Rachel Toor.
Other titles: Chicago guides to writing, editing, and publishing.
Description: Chicago : The University of Chicago Press, 2017.
Identifiers: LCCN 2016053327 | ISBN 9780226383750 (cloth : alk. paper) | ISBN 9780226383897 (pbk. : alk. paper) | ISBN 9780226383927 (e-book)
Subjects: LCSH: College applications—United States. | Universities and colleges—United States—Admission. | Creative writing. | Essay—Authorship.
Classification: LCC LB2351.5 .T66 2017 | DDC 378.1/616—dc23
LC record available at https://lccn.loc.gov/2016053327

♾ This paper meets the requirements of ANSI/NISO Z39.48-1992 (Permanence of Paper).

CONTENTS

Part Two

INTRODUCTION

The Quest for the Special Secret Sauce

When Daniel's dad wrote to ask me to help his son with his college admissions essay, I wanted to say no. I had stopped doing that kind of work. Then I learned that Daniel, a first-generation Chinese American, attended the exam-entrance public boarding school where I had, years before, coached cross country for a season.

Here's a confession. I was a crappy coach. Even though I'd run fifty or sixty marathons and even longer races, I had never been on a team, had never run cross country, and had no idea how meets were scored. I got the job because the school was desperate; I interviewed in the morning and met with the team that afternoon.

As it turned out, I adored coaching, but I didn't give a hoot if my team won or lost. I wanted the students to love running as much as I did. I had left my job as an admissions officer at Duke University and had published a book called *Admissions Confidential: An Insider's Account of the Elite College Admissions Process*. Though I no longer worked in admissions, I wanted to help my runners think about their college applications and to share with them what I thought they needed to know.

More than a dozen years later, when Daniel's dad contacted me, I was trying to write a novel set in a school like the one where I'd briefly worked. I told Daniel's dad that while I no longer did college counseling, I had an idea for an exchange of services: I would help Daniel with his essays if he'd read a draft of my novel and give me critical feedback. Daniel said sure.

Daniel was at the top of his class, had perfect SAT scores and 5s on his many AP tests, was Student Senate president, was captain of the Science Bowl, played trombone, and did immunology research in the department of surgery at Duke. I knew he would be a strong applicant.

And he had already done a lot of work. Daniel sent me drafts of polished essays. He wrote his Common App essay about taking walks with his grandfather when he was nine. His Yale short-answer supplement provided an account of how he had lobbied his school to serve healthier food in the cafeteria. Here's the email I sent after reading his drafts.

Daniel,

What I believe about writing is that we all pretty much know what's wrong with our own work. We convince ourselves what we've written is okay because it's so hard to write well and we want to be done. Or we decide that maybe no one else will notice the problems.

Let me be clear: there's nothing wrong with these essays. If I were to rate them on a scale of 1 to 5 (as admissions officers do), they'd each get a 3. They're fine. You've clearly worked very hard on these. But a different kind of work is required when you write in the first-person personal.

These essays are generic and cliché—exactly as you feared. The problems might be less the topic than your approach, which feels like you're trying to write what you think "they" want to read. The best essays are rarely about how students have succeeded or achieved. You have your teachers and your list of activities for that. Excellent essays show the reader how you've struggled, or describe mistakes you've made. They express what you're fired up about, how you think, and show the ways you've grown—stuff that's small and close, rather than big, sweeping "this is how great I am" kinds of things. Your Yale supplement doesn't do much to let me know who you are as a person. I could get everything I need from the essay in one sentence: "I'm a leader." That message will come through in the other parts of your application.

The Common App essay, while admirably polished, falls fully into the "dead grandparent" cliché (I wrote my own Yale application essay about my dead grandma, but it was a lot easier to get in back then). I'm more interested in who you are now—your intellectual interests, your passions, your family, your quirks, the things that make you who you are and not what happened when you were nine.

There are nearly 30,000 kids applying to Yale. Most of them are more than qualified to get in. They tend to look identical in terms of test scores, grades, courses taken, extracurricular activities. The admissions officers have to wade through piles of files. Think about what you can say that will interest an exhausted reader. How can you reveal yourself in ways that will make her want to argue to admit you instead of the 29,999 other applicants? A good essay will be conversational, rich in vivid and specific details, and could only be written by one person—you. In your unique voice. I'm not getting that from these.

It's up to you to decide what you want to do. I'm willing to work with you, but as I told your dad, I see my job as teaching kids how to write better, not just coming up with an essay for a college application.

Best,
Rachel

Daniel spent the next month writing draft after draft. I promised I'd always tell him the truth, even if it was hard to hear. He listened, learned, and revised.

His final essays were honest, authentic, revealing, and funny. He wrote about his struggles with zits. Yes, friends, Daniel wrote about pimples. So much better than his braggy *I am a leader!* essay.

At the end of our work together, Daniel sent me an email.

Dear Rachel,

Over the past few weeks I had kind of an "existential awakening," and I realized that for these past few years I had focused nearly all of my time on doing things that would help me get into college, and everything that I had done, whether consciously or subliminally, could be rationalized based on the fact that it would help me get into college, prepare me for future success, etc.

Which is not to say that I didn't enjoy what I did, because I did enjoy the activities I did, but it's more that I think the atmosphere at school turned me into a sort of robot—I was doing a bunch of things, but I never reflected on why I did the things I did. Everyone here is so focused on success and achievement, and people compete rigorously for it and judge each other based on each other's accomplishments, and I realized that I had been sucked into that culture.

But now I've begun to realize how meaningless and unauthentic that culture really is, and that success and achievement really aren't as important as we make them seem to be. I think what's more important is connecting with and caring for other people, both on an individual level and on a societal level. And promoting social justice, because we've been fortunate to even think about attending top-tier institutions and not have to worry about surviving day to day. I think that's a much more meaningful goal for life than just trying to get into college (though much easier said than done).

Daniel

Daniel ended up at Yale. He may well have been admitted if he hadn't rewritten his essays. The truth is, I didn't care where he went to college; I knew he'd do fine anywhere. I wanted him to learn about writing well and to use the process to think hard about himself. As you can see, he did.

Writing Is Hard and Scary—for Everyone

I know what you really want from this book: the recipe for the special secret sauce for the college application essay. If you add these ingredients together and mix, your application will be accepted.

Did you notice how I phrased that? I did not say *you* would be accepted. Nor did I say *you* would be rejected. Admissions professionals are not judging your value as a person, though I know it can feel that way. Students often fear that if they reveal any perceived failings—that they got a C in physics, that they misspelled *misspelled* on an eighth-grade test, that they challenged their teachers when asked to recite the Pledge of Allegiance or got caught with beer on a field trip—they're going to blow their chances of gaining admission. Not so.

Like Daniel, high-achieving high school students tend

> Don't try to figure out what other people want to hear from you; figure out what you have to say. It's the one and only thing you have to offer.
>
> BARBARA KINGSOLVER

to suffer from the disease of perfectionism. But anyone who has ever has studied art or watched *America's Next Top Model* knows that beauty comes from flaws, imperfections, oddities.

Hear this: You are not perfect. You will never be perfect.

Thank goodness.

And if you're not one of those kids whose hand is first to shoot into the air anytime the teacher asks a question, if you've only recently begun to care about grades or didn't think college was an option, let me tell you this: it's never too late to become a good student or writer.

You already have the most important ingredient: your unique personality. No matter what the assignment, being yourself on the page is the most effective move. Use words you actually say every day, not brand-new ones suggested by a thesaurus. Be funny if you're funny, and if you're not, don't try to make jokes. Good writing is about voice—your voice. Don't contort yourself to sound like someone else.

Easy, right?

Wrong.

It's hard.

Let's face it. Writing, for most of us, is bound up with anxiety.

As soon as we learn to talk, we're made aware of our many mistakes. From our parents and our teachers, even from some of our friends, we receive correction. The intentions are good; the resulting shame can be crippling. Papers are returned bleeding red ink with comments like

Awkward, *Unclear*, and *????*. Spelling errors get circled, grammar fixed, syntax mended. The act of finishing an essay you've worked hard on seems a triumph, but then you show it to someone else—someone who cares about you and wants you to succeed—and it can feel like they are demolishing your effort by exposing your shortcomings. Sometimes you just want to give up.

We are taught rules and regulations. We learn that every essay must have an introduction, three body paragraphs, and a conclusion. It needs to have a thesis. Don't use contractions. No sentence fragments. No split infinitives—we're not supposed to boldly go where no one has gone before. Ending on a preposition is something up with which the authorities will not put. And you can't begin a sentence with a conjunction like *and* or *but* or *because*.

It's scary. And amazing that anyone can get over the fear of judgment long enough to write even one sentence. When it feels like your whole future—or at least where you'll spend the next four years of college—is on the line, it's easy to understand why so many high school seniors put off writing their essay until the last minute. It would be more fun to clean the toilet with a toothbrush, less stressful to walk a tightrope over the Grand Canyon.

Personal writing can be even scarier. In a good college application essay you seek to expose yourself in ways that are honest and intimate and compelling. This is not your standard five-paragraph essay—in fact, in many ways it may be the opposite of what you've been taught in high school. You may need to unlearn, or relearn, some stuff.

Personal essays are different from the analytical papers you are asked to write for academic classes. The thesis of every personal essay can be reduced to "This is who I am." Or maybe "Why I'm like this." Instead of seeking to answer a question or prove a point, a good personal essay does the opposite. It looks at complexities. It opens out into more

> Use the time of a total stranger in such a way that he or she will not feel the time was wasted.
>
> KURT VONNEGUT

questions. It wonders. It wanders. Wrote poet Walt Whitman: "Do I contradict myself? / Very well then, I contradict myself. / (I am large, I contain multitudes.)" Instead of shrinking yourself down to a simplistic stick figure ("I am a leader"; "I love football"), you need to show the many facets of you, the multitudes.

Your essay can zig and zag. It can be about something as mundane as zits. Staying small and close to your own experience is more valuable than pronouncing on the Problem in Society Today. A good essay often starts with a question, where you go, "Hmmm. I wonder what's up with ____." It could be kidneys. Why do we have two kidneys and only one heart? How you puzzle through that question will tell readers much about you and how you think. Or, "Can you be a feminist if you enjoy *The Bachelor*?" A good essay doesn't have to answer questions; it just needs to raise them in interesting ways.

Even though it's the job of overworked admissions officers to read your application, it's in your interest to make their labor enjoyable. In this book I'll tell you about bad decisions beginning writers make and how to avoid them. I'll remind you not to get too attached to your own work; you must be willing to revise, because that's the most important part of writing. I'll give you tips to make your sentences stronger and strategies to cut needless words.

And, at a stressful time in your life, I will ask you to do something terrifying: to reveal the weakest, most vulnerable parts of yourself. When you might be tempted to boast about your achievements, I'm going to ask you to think about your failures. If you can say the hardest thing about yourself, instead of being judged and rejected you will be applauded for your honesty and your bravery. I want you to be honest and brave.

I'm here to tell you there is no special secret sauce for the application essay. Or, rather, the most important ingredient in the sauce is you. If you can figure out how to present yourself well on the page, someone will fall in love with you. And that's what it's all about.

What to Write About?

Once you commit the time and the emotional energy to get your butt in the chair to write, you face the next daunting task: figuring out what to write about. If you're stuck, you're in good company. This is a challenge for most students.

You may be unaccustomed to so many degrees of freedom. You get to choose a topic about which you are the expert. Your parents. Your favorite place. That time you struck out in the championship game. Your bad skin. Your dog. Your first love. (Or even your first love: your dog.) This isn't an English paper on some "classic" novel that you didn't like and couldn't even finish. If you approach the task by spewing out a bunch of words you found in the thesaurus about concepts you barely understand, you're not doing anyone any favors. As much as you hate writing those essays, people hate having to read them even more.

Unique ideas are hard to come by. If you rely on a gimmick, it will fail, as surely as if you try too hard to do something that's never been done before. *Hey*, you might think, *I bet no one has ever written about being chased by a potbellied pig*. Wrong. I've read that essay (loved it).

The best topic is one that you really want to write about. If the topic doesn't matter to you, believe me, it won't matter to the reader. It's not what you write about as much as how you approach your subject matter.

You might decide to do an essay about being a middle child. You're not the only middle child in the world, but each middle child can write a different essay. You may experience similar struggles (never getting to be the first at anything; being the peacemaker), but the particulars are going to be different. Tolstoy famously started his great novel *Anna Karenina* with the line "Happy families are all alike; every unhappy family is unhappy in its own way." That doesn't mean you have to come from an unhappy family in order to be able to write a good essay. But even if your family gets along like a litter of Labrador puppies, someone will occasionally step on a tail or bite too hard.

Here's another tip: a good topic is usually what I call "both/and" rather than "either/or." In high school, you may have been encouraged to write papers that took a side: Either you are for the death penalty or you're against it. Either *Uncle Tom's Cabin* was the most important American novel ever or it's sentimental drivel. Either/or is okay in academic papers when you're arguing for a specific position, but in a personal essay, both/and is better. It allows you to express clashing feelings and explore them. You are for the death penalty *and* some aspects of it make you queasy. Both/and, not either/or.

Conflict is useful, inevitable, and essential. The sixteenth-century philosopher Michel de Montaigne, from whom we get the word *essay* (*essai*, in French, means to attempt or to try), wrote, "There is no conversation more boring than the one where everybody agrees." So "I love my mom" does not make for a good essay. "I love my mom even though she makes me clean my room, hates my guinea pig, and is crazy about disgusting food like kale" could lead somewhere.

Remember: You're Writing for Humans

Picture this before you plop yourself down in front of your computer.

A winter-lit room is crammed with a group of people that include admissions officers, the dean of admissions, and in some cases a bunch of harried faculty members. They sit around a big table covered with files. The admissions professionals, often young and underpaid, will be nicely dressed, with shiny hair and gobs of enthusiasm, and the professors will frequently pause to take off their glasses and rub their eyes. These exhausted folks have been sitting in committee meetings for days, after they've spent a couple of months reading applications, most of which look pretty darn similar.

It's late afternoon. They're hangry. Or they're hopped up from eating too many cookies and brownies brought in by admissions officers, who know that treats can, um, encourage people to go along with their recommendations. They wade through long lists of candidates, state by state, region by region. The very best applications and the weakest don't come to committee. They're already in or they're out. It's the gigantic stack in the middle that warrants discussion.

The admissions officer responsible for your region gets to your application and reads from her notes. She introduces you to the committee. She'll say, "This is [your first name here], a straight-A student from [your high school here], who maxed out her curriculum by taking 5 AP courses and getting 4s on all the tests. She plays the tuba, has a job harvesting bat guano, and is the founder of the Cheez-It Lovers Club." She talks about your course selection, your grades, and your test scores. She'll use shorthand jargon to describe your more typical achievements and extracurricular activities. Then she'll talk about what you've written.

Some time ago my friend Owen, a professor of computer science at Duke and one of the best teachers I know, gave me some excellent advice. He said, "I teach in slogans. If you give people catchy phrases that capture big ideas, they're more likely to remember them." So now I too teach in slogans, some of which you'll find repeated throughout this book:

» Steal, steal, steal

» Read greedy, not grouchy

» Write like the best, smartest version of yourself

» A good essay is not about what it's about

» Find your pirates

» Tell a story, have some thoughts

» Fill the hole in your donut

» Murder your darlings

» Both/and is more interesting than either/or

» Don't try to hook the reader like a trout

» When the action is hot, write cool

» Failure is gold

» Good stuff in, good stuff out

» The reader is always in it for herself

» All good writing is vivid and specific

» It's not what you write about, it's how you do it

» Show the cunning of the innocent and the loneliness of the monster

» Stay small and close; take small bites out of big issues

» Say the hardest thing

» Clichés think your thoughts for you

» Be generous to everyone, including your past self

» A piece of writing often does not start where it starts

» Go to the shame

» Revise using a new blank document

» Paragraph breaks are your—and your readers'—friends

» Read it out loud

When I worked in admissions at Duke, my favorite part of the job was finding essays I couldn't wait to share. I'd tear down the hall to find a colleague to whom I could say, "Check out this baseball player who wrote about sitting on the pitcher's mound and thinking." Or "You have to read what this Math Olympiad girl said about *Hamlet*." Often another admissions officer would wave a file in front of me saying, "You, my friend, are going to love this kid."

In committee meetings, when someone started to talk

about a great essay, I'd reach over the cookies to grab the file so I could read it. The fact is, most essays were typical. Many were boring. Some were just plain bad. The good ones I remembered. After I read a really good one I'd send a postcard to the applicant—well before the notification date—saying how much I enjoyed his or her essay. (If you get such a note, you can pretty much count on being admitted.)

Admissions essays are personal for the applicant, and also for those who review them. It might be easier to write an essay if you think no one will ever read it. That's a recipe for a piece of work that speaks to, well, no one. All writing is a public performance, unless you're penning journal entries. Good writers know they have to think about the reader. I want you to go into this process armed with the information you need to write an essay that will make admissions officers jump out of their chairs and say, "We have got to admit this kid!"

This Book

As I'll explain in depth later, often an early draft of an essay doesn't start where it starts. In this book I want to teach you how to write your way in to an essay that matters. If you can do that, you may well end up writing your way into the hearts and minds of the admissions officers who will read it, love it, and then act as your lobbyists on the committee.

Plenty of books and websites give examples of "essays that worked." I find that silly, and often a case of confusing correlation with causation. Just because an applicant was admitted, you can't infer that her essay was stellar. Some of those models are no better than mediocre. I've chosen not to include any complete essays in this book, because I don't think reading them is a good use of your time. Instead I'll show you how to write your own excellent and unforgettable essay. I'll also share with you stories of real students I've worked with so you can see how they learned to solve problems everyone encounters. And I've included quotations from some of my favorite writers throughout the book to show you how even the great ones struggle.

Now, slogging through a whole book—even a short one—just to write a 650-word composition might seem like overkill. My goal here is to reduce your stress level, to teach you about the genre of the personal essay, but most important, to provide you with skills that will be useful once you're in college and afterward. The ability to write well may be the most valuable and marketable skill you can acquire, one that too few people possess. If you're freaked out, join the club. Most people are called on to write in the first person only for high-stakes assignments: applications to college (and to graduate and professional schools); cover letters for jobs; self-assessments for promotion; grant applications; online dating profiles.

Here's some good news. The essay is the one part of the application that is completely within your control. By writing something that reflects the real you, you can feel satisfied that your college acceptance comes, as they say on my favorite TV show, for the right reasons. (Rejections, however, often stem from other sources: too many strong applicants from northern New Jersey; the orchestra didn't need another oboe player; your parents forgot to donate millions of dollars to the college.)

Even though I'm no longer a college counselor, I still get asked for help, and when I was in the throes of finishing up the manuscript for this book, I started working with Michael, the gazillionth member of a big extended family I've been working with for more than a decade. I told him he had to read the entire manuscript before I'd look at one word of his essay. I also asked him for feedback on how to make it better.

Michael, a sophisticated reader who attended an excellent high school and who watched his siblings and cousins go through this process, said he found the chapters at the end of the book the most helpful. He liked the warnings, the reminders about technical aspects of writing, the ways to think about revision, the tips. The early parts didn't feel as relevant as he struggled to get a draft of an essay done.

That's fine. Read this book however it is most useful to you. If you're the student who asks, "Do I have to know this for the test?," you may want to read part 2 first. If you're stressed and worried about getting the whole college application ordeal over with, it may be hard to sit through big-picture stuff before you get to practical nuts-and-bolts advice you can put to immediate use. But when I started reading Michael's work, I discovered he hadn't fully grasped some of the most important points I make in part 1. His initial list of topics was too typical; he hadn't understood that failure is gold, that happy families are all alike, and that if he didn't really care about the topic, neither would his reader. When I reminded him of this, he came up with a much better list and, ultimately, a great essay (about his passion for the Boston Celtics).

Good writing needs to be mechanically correct and insightful, concise and specific. Your essay, based on personal experience, must touch on a universal feeling. That's what I'll try to convince you of in part 1. After you understand what an essay is and what it has to do (which may surprise you), I'll show you, in part 2, with specific and pragmatic tips, how to polish it so it shines.

You can do this. I promise.

It might even be fun.

Part One

WHAT YOU NEED TO KNOW BEFORE YOU START WRITING

1
Steal, Steal, Steal

LEARNING TO READ LIKE A WRITER

Let's start with a harsh but simple truth: if you don't like to read, no one will want to read what you write. That includes your college application essay.

And if you're about to argue that you read all the time, that you have stacks of the latest zombie/apocalypse/vampire novels on your night table, I'm going to counter that there is a difference between reading good stuff and bingeing on junk.

Don't get me wrong. I'm a huge consumer of junk in a variety of forms. Here, as always, I am a proponent of both/and. I'm always reading something "good"—a book by Joan Didion or Chimamanda Ngozi Adichie, writers whose sentences are crafted with such care and skill you can't but savor each one—and also, usually before I go to sleep, a mystery novel whose twisty plot keeps me awake too late.

My e-reader is filled with more novels than I could consume in five lifetimes. I always have a mess of audiobooks from the library in my car, and when I go for long runs, I bring my iPod loaded with books. I once accidentally ran for five hours because I could not stop listening to Zadie Smith's novel *On Beauty*. Yes, I think listening to books counts as reading. And yes, you can accidentally run for five hours. Or at least I can, if the book is great.

Perhaps you've heard the computer science acronym

GIGO: garbage in, garbage out. The corollary is "good stuff in, good stuff out." If your output is writing, your input is reading. So before we delve into the writing, I'm going to show you what it's like to read as a writer.

Sentences That Give You Chills

Writers read differently from other people. Unlike researchers, writers don't read only for content. While your English teachers may talk about symbolism and meaning and catharsis and onomatopoeia, I have never heard one living writer mention any of those when she's discussing her own work. Writers talk less about *what* other authors do than they wonder *how* they do it. When we study how excellent writers construct their essays, we do so to learn useful tips for crafting our own. We are constantly on the lookout for moves and tricks we can steal to use in our own work.

Understand that I'm not telling you to commit plagiarism. Passing off someone else's words as your own is a crime, like writing a bad check or cooking up a batch of meth. You have to use your own words and ideas, but what you can lift from other writers is the way they structure their essays, or their use of lists, or even how they put the parts of their sentences together.

In every class I teach I say, "Good writers steal, steal, steal." I say the word three times to make sure my students get the point, and then I show them how to read for theft-worthy moves and tricks.

In one class, however, I made this pronouncement and the students, all grown men, looked at each other, looked at me, and then started laughing so hard I thought they would give themselves hernias. I'd never had a reaction like that before. A few days later I talked this over with a friend and her son, a cop. He started sniggering and asked me, again, where I was teaching.

> The Six Golden Rules of Writing: Read, read, read, and write, write, write.
>
> ERNEST GAINES

Then it hit me: Airway Heights Correctional Center is a medium-security men's prison. Many of these guys had probably been sent to the pokey for larceny.

In the next class I decided to show those giggling inmates what I meant. I had them read Martin Luther King Jr.'s "Letter from a Birmingham Jail," which he first wrote on scraps of paper in a cell during the civil rights movement of the 1960s.

We spent a lot of time talking about Dr. King's prose, about its rhythm and musical beauty, how the sounds amplify the sense. We marveled at balanced parallel constructions like this one: "If I have said anything in this letter that is an understatement of the truth and is indicative of an unreasonable impatience, I beg you to forgive me. If I have said anything in this letter that is an overstatement of the truth and is indicative of my having a patience that makes me patient with anything less than brotherhood, I beg God to forgive me."

We talked about how Dr. King builds his argument, how he comes up with every objection readers could have to his statements, presents the best case for their side, and then shows, with examples from history and from the Bible, why and how they are wrong. If you want to make a convincing argument, instead of ridiculing or caricaturing the opposition's points (creating an easily knocked-over "straw man"), you make the strongest argument against your own position and engage with that. You do this in order to be persuasive, and also because it's playing fair.

Another stealable trick from Dr. King's essay can be

summarized with a slogan I've stolen from a writer friend: *When the action is hot, write cool.* If you scream at the top of your lungs, you'll sound like a crazy person. If you use inflammatory rhetoric to describe a desperate situation, it will be easy for your listeners to turn away and dismiss your concerns. When you're furious with someone, instead of yelling and stabbing your finger into their chest, if you quietly and calmly explain yourself, hands clasped politely in your lap, you will be more effective.

I also encourage students to steal from Dr. King's essay the use of a periodic sentence. There's a fancy grammatical explanation for what that is, but let's just say it's a sentence where you as the reader don't know what the action is until you get to the end. It's basically a bunch of dependent clauses waiting for a verb. Many sentences start with a subject and a verb at the beginning and then get longer by adding clauses, one after the next. (In that example, the subject and verb are *sentences start.*) In a periodic sentence, the verb comes at the end.

In the "Letter," Dr. King responds to the moderate white clergymen who have been urging him to slow down his efforts at integration. We're on your side, they have told him, but really, it would be better for everyone if you wait. He writes, "Perhaps it is easy for those who have never felt the stinging darts of segregation to say, 'Wait.'" Then continues,

> But when you have seen vicious mobs lynch your mothers and fathers at will and drown your sisters and brothers at whim; when you have seen hate filled policemen curse, kick and even kill your black brothers and sisters; when you see the vast majority of your twenty million Negro brothers smothering in an airtight cage of poverty in the midst of an affluent society; when

you suddenly find your tongue twisted and your speech stammering as you seek to explain to your six year old daughter why she can't go to the public amusement park that has just been advertised on television, and see tears welling up in her eyes when she is told that Funtown is closed to colored children, and see ominous clouds of inferiority beginning to form in her little mental sky, and see her beginning to distort her personality by developing an unconscious bitterness toward white people; when you have to concoct an answer for a five year old son who is asking: "Daddy, why do white people treat colored people so mean?"; when you take a cross county drive and find it necessary to sleep night after night in the uncomfortable corners of your automobile because no motel will accept you; when you are humiliated day in and day out by nagging signs reading "white" and "colored"; when your first name becomes "nigger," your middle name becomes "boy" (however old you are) and your last name becomes "John," and your wife and mother are never given the respected title "Mrs."; when you are harried by day and haunted by night by the fact that you are a Negro, living constantly at tiptoe stance, never quite knowing what to expect next, and are plagued with inner fears and outer resentments; when you are forever fighting a degenerating sense of "nobodiness"—then you will understand why we find it difficult to wait.

Even though I've dissected that sentence seven thousand times, I still get chills whenever I read it. Read it aloud and tell me you don't get chills. Do you see what Dr. King is doing? With his sentence structure, he allows us to grasp how African Americans suffered during segregation. He gives us vivid and specific examples of the dehumanizing experiences of real people, and he uses the sentence structure to make us wait, and wait, and wait, as they have waited, to be treated as equals.

If you take out all those dependent clauses, the sentence would read, "But when you have seen what I've seen, you will understand why we find it difficult to wait." That's a vague sentence many of us might be tempted to write. We assume the reader will trust us and don't feel like we have to explain ourselves. That impulse is almost always wrong. You can see from Dr. King's example how much power you gain by using concrete examples. I plan to hammer into you the idea that good writing is always vivid and specific.

Good stuff in, good stuff out.

Read Greedy, Not Grouchy

Now, you may have been so enchanted by Dr. King's sentence that you dropped this book, googled "Letter from a Birmingham Jail," and read the entire essay already. (I hope so.) Or you may have taken one look at the big block of text, gotten a headache, and skipped to this section. If you skipped ahead, please go back. I promise the view will be worth the climb.

And even if you don't like that sentence, surely you will see how you can learn from Dr. King's example. That's one of the most important aspects of reading like a writer. You don't have to enjoy something in order to be able to steal from it. It's natural to complain about being forced to read

> The greatest part of a writer's time is spent in reading, in order to write; a man will turn over half a library to make one book.
>
> SAMUEL JOHNSON

stuff for school when you know what you like and that's what you want to read. You may have thought *A Tale of Two Cities* was the longest, most boring book in the history of the world and you can count the ways you hated it. You're happier curled up with J. K. Rowling or John Green.

While understandable, that's not a winning strategy. Some books and essays will speak more directly to you than others. Some will make you feel like the writer sawed open your head and heart, understood the contents, and expressed your feelings and ideas in ways you never could. That's what we hope for when we read. But sometimes, well, a piece of work everyone agrees is Great Literature isn't your thing. No problem. If you read lots of books, you won't love them all. But it behooves you to figure out why other people like them and think they're good and worthwhile.

Often we dislike things that seem hard. In college I complained when I had to slog through John Milton's epic poem *Paradise Lost*. I spent more time telling my friends how much I hated that book than I did reading it. Then I went into class and the teacher explained that she viewed Satan as a tragic hero. She quoted the poet William Blake, who said that God-fearing Milton "was of the Devil's party without realizing it." How cool is that? Now, when students whine about having to read *Paradise Lost* for their lit classes, I recite Satan's speech at the end of book 1 and show them how it's the best down-at-the-half locker-room pep talk in the history of English literature. *Oh*, they say. *I didn't get that*.

Be patient when you struggle with a book. If you're confused about why anyone else might think a piece of writing is good—if you'd rather watch paint dry than turn another page of *Pride and Prejudice* or *Catcher in the Rye*—ask a teacher, or a parent, or a friend what you might be missing. People are always happy to talk about what they love.

Where should you look for examples of good personal essays?

You can find tons of websites that collect them. Google "best personal essays" and you'll discover treasures. Pick up a book from the annual series called *Best American Essays*. There's also a yearly *Best American Nonrequired Reading*, whose entries are selected by high school students, and Best American writing collections on sports, travel, science, and nature. Each week the *New Yorker* magazine publishes great writing on subjects you had no idea you'd find fascinating. Ask your teachers and parents and librarians for recommendations. Especially librarians. They are great sources of information and generous, helpful people.

Read essays about topics you're interested in, or by writers who speak to you, and then figure out which techniques you can steal. Learn to mark what I call the "gold star sentence"—a sentence you love so much you wish you had written it. Start a collection of good sentences.

In my classes we'll read Joan Didion's essay "On Going Home" and notice how she employs the passive voice—often a bad choice, but so useful here—to show the docility she feels when she visits her family. We'll look at how Eula Biss uses the visual imagery of the telephone pole to think about the history of lynching in "Time and Distance Overcome." Nora Ephron's "What I Wish I'd Known" is a list of funny pieces of advice that somehow manages to add up to more than the sum of its parts. In Malcolm Gladwell's "Six Degrees of Lois Weisberg," he braids a profile of a grandmotherly woman in Chicago into a lively narrative that includes academic research about how we are connected to other people. Ann Hood's essay "Comfort" trots out a bunch of clichés to show the grating uselessness of people's attempts to console her after the death of her five-year-old daughter. Each of these techniques can be stolen.

An essay I always give my students is Robert Kurson's "My Favorite Teacher," about his experience as an awkward high school student whose favorite teacher turned out to be raping and murdering boys. Kurson is able to weave together several different threads: his own alienated experience in high school, the misdeeds of an adored teacher, and his quest, later in life, to figure out how a monstrous man could have been so important to him. It's the both/and aspect of this relationship that makes the essay so complex and rich.

I also ask students to read Debra Dickerson's "Who Shot Johnny?," which begins with a cool and detached tone:

> Given my level of political awareness, it was inevitable that I would come to view the everyday events of my life through the prism of politics and the national discourse. I read *The Washington Post*, *The New Republic*, *The New Yorker*, *Harper's*, *The Atlantic Monthly*, *The Nation*, *National Review*, *Black Enterprise*, and *Essence* and wrote a weekly column for the Harvard Law School *Record* during my three years just ended there. I do this because I know that those of us who are not well-fed white guys in suits must not yield the debate to them, however well-intentioned or well-informed they may be. Accordingly, I am unrepentant and vocal about having gained admittance to Harvard through affirmative action; I am a feminist, stoic about my marriage chances as a well-educated, thirty-six-year-old black woman who won't pretend to need help taking care of herself.

She goes on to describe time spent in the hospital with her nephew, the victim of a drive-by shooting, and ends here:

> Alone, lying in the road bleeding and paralyzed but hideously conscious, Johnny had lain helpless as he watched his would-be murderer come to stand over him and offer this prophecy: "Betch'ou won't be doin' nomo' wavin,' mothafucker."
>
> Fuck you, asshole. He's fine from the waist up. You just can't do anything right, can you?

We read to figure out how she managed that tonal shift, how she earned the right to end the essay as she did, the most effective way I can imagine.

Learn to read greedy instead of grouchy. Read a lot, and read lots of different kinds of things. You're looking for stuff to steal.

2
Craft Your "I"

THINKING OF YOURSELF AS A CHARACTER

George Orwell, whom you may know as the author of the novels *Animal Farm* and *1984*, wrote many beautifully crafted essays with plenty of steal-worthy moves. His "Shooting an Elephant" begins:

> In Moulmein, in lower Burma, I was hated by large numbers of people—the only time in my life that I have been important enough for this to happen to me.

Here we have a man who presents himself as a bit of a bumbler with a wry and self-deprecating sense of humor. Orwell spends a couple of paragraphs on the decline of the British Empire. He explains why imperialism is bad and then launches in with this:

> One day something happened which in a roundabout way was enlightening. It was a tiny incident in itself, but it gave me a better glimpse than I had had before of the real nature of imperialism—the real motives for which despotic governments act.

This is Orwell the novelist ready to launch into a story. He uses his skills as a fiction writer to bring us into a place, introduce us to characters, create tension, and, most importantly, to make us feel. Every time I read the essay I have to skim over the scene where Orwell shoots the elephant that terrorized a community and killed a person. The writer makes us cry for the death of the poor animal, but when he recounts how a Burmese man was trampled to death, his description is merely grotesque. He makes his point about how colonialism dehumanizes both intellectually and emotionally and implicates the reader, who realizes how misplaced her sympathies are. (Google "Shooting an Elephant." Read it. Trust me.)

It feels like a different person altogether wrote "Politics and the English Language," which opens with this:

> Most people who bother with the matter at all would admit that the English language is in a bad way, but it is generally assumed that we cannot by conscious action do anything about it. Our civilization is decadent and our language—so the argument runs—must inevitably share in the general collapse.

This Orwell is self-assured and is about to tell us, in the way of many essays written by students, "what's wrong with society today." He goes on to say, specifically and via a handful of short examples so awful they're painful to read, how the English language is degraded and abused by politicians and professors. In the essay he gives a good set of reminders on how to write better, and even more important, he lays out what is at stake when we write badly. Hint: it's the rise of totalitarianism. (Google "Politics and the English Language." Read it. Trust me.)

In these two essays Orwell deploys different strategies. In each he introduces himself in a manner that will allow him to accomplish what he sets out to do. We can imagine the Orwell of "Politics and the English Language" in a tweed jacket standing at a lectern. The Orwell who wrote "Shooting an Elephant" sits in a pub nursing a beer.

You, too, have different identities, and for each essay you get to figure out which one to bring to the task.

Write like the Best, Smartest Version of Yourself

The greatest compliment you can receive as a writer is when someone reads your work and says, "That sounds just like you."

When you write about yourself in the first person, you strive to be the best, smartest, most interesting version of your true self. You write in a natural fashion without strain or artifice. You don't try to hide your flaws, and you don't undersell your sterling qualities; you report on yourself as objectively as you can. You're not afraid to go to a place of shame and look at it without judgment. You don't tell the reader what to think; you bring him along with you as you explore an idea or topic.

Oh great, you say. How am I supposed to do that?

At this point, you've sat through hours of English class discussions about fictional characters. You may have talked about how Nick Carraway, the narrator of *The Great Gatsby*, isn't the protagonist of the book. Or is he? Is Hester Prynn a victim of slut-shaming? How do the things surrounding a character—the objects, the habits—make the person come to life, like Sherlock Holmes's pipe and his taste for cocaine?

You've learned a lot about characters and characterization in literature classes and by watching movies. But think about this: each time you write "I" in any context, you create a character. Like Orwell, you contain within you many facets. You are a musician. You are a baseball player. You are a girl who loves pigs. You are a math whiz. You are a lazy

> Write as if you were dying. At the same time, assume you write for an audience consisting solely of terminal patients. That is, after all, the case. What would you begin writing if you knew you would die soon? What could you say to a dying person that would not enrage by its triviality?
>
> ANNIE DILLARD

reality-TV addict. You are a consumer of massive quantities of chocolate. You are a good big brother. You are a mean big brother. You are a quiet student. You are a boisterous friend. You carry around many selves. Writing an essay requires you to pick one of these characters to craft on the page.

When you write to your parents, your I is that of a kid, no matter, I'm sorry to say, how old you are. When you write to your teachers, you do not—please, I beg you—address them in the same way you would your friends. If you write a fan letter to your favorite author (my email is racheltoor@gmail.com, just saying), you might introduce yourself differently from the way you would if you were applying for a job at Starbucks or talking to a neighbor who's known you your whole life.

We call each of these various forms of "I" a persona. Think about Stephen Colbert, a comedian who created a talk-show-host character also named "Stephen Colbert" in a parody of political commentators. While the two Colberts had some things in common, the version on *The Colbert Report* was deployed to satirize. Or consider this: Stefani Germanotta was a dedicated, disciplined student; her persona Lady Gaga got the attention of the world through outrageous costumes and behavior, not to mention some serious musical chops.

One of my favorite examples of persona in writing is Jonathan Swift's 1729 essay "A Modest Proposal." Here Swift, the author of *Gulliver's Travels*, an Anglican clergyman, takes on the manner of a gentleman much concerned about Ireland's poor children: *we have too many babies, and people are starving*. He writes,

> I think it is agreed by all parties, that this prodigious number of children in the arms, or on the backs, or at the heels of their mothers, and frequently of their fathers, is in the present deplorable state of the kingdom, a very great additional grievance; and therefore whoever could find out a fair, cheap and easy method of making these children sound and useful members of the common-wealth, would deserve so well of the publick, as to have his statue set up for a preserver of the nation.

After he explains the problem, Swift's narrator, in his sophisticated and gentlemanly voice, says, "I shall now therefore humbly propose my own thoughts, which I hope will not be liable to the least objection."

We're eager to know what this calm, reasonable man proposes. Are you ready? Here it is:

> I have been assured by a very knowing American of my acquaintance in London, that a young healthy child well nursed, is, at a year old, a most delicious nourishing and wholesome food, whether stewed, roasted, baked, or boiled; and I make no doubt that it will equally serve in a fricassee, or a ragout.

And there you have it. The poor of Ireland are starving? I know. Let's eat the babies!

Swift lays out an argument for exactly how and why

this solution should work. It's brilliant and the reasoning is flawless. Except for one small matter. This modest proposal is, of course, completely immoral, a fact that Swift the writer is well aware of, but that his helpful narrator—the persona—pretends to ignore, all the better to make a point about the failures of governance faced by the Irish and the burdens placed on its poor.

Persona isn't always such an exaggeration. It's more an aspect of your real self that speaks for a particular occasion. If you're writing a letter to a friend about your little brother and how he drives you nuts, you may indulge in some big-sisterly trash talk and call him a "bratty little douchebag." If you're writing for a teacher, however, you might say he's a "stubborn child."

An Example Involving Another Swift

It might help to think about persona like an outfit. In the summer of 2015 I was lucky enough to see Taylor Swift in concert. She strutted on a runway in a glittery cheerleader skirt and crop top and belted out "Welcome to New York." For "Trouble" and "I Wish You Would" she looked smoking hot in a black leather bra and bun-huggers. But for "How You Get the Girl," she changed into a flirty pink dress. At the end of the show she came out in a long gown to shake it off. Each of these songs represented a different aspect of Taylor Swift. Each change of clothes fit the singer of that particular song—same person, different personas.

In case you're interested, the concert was a blast. But

> Most of the basic material a writer works with is acquired before the age of fifteen.
>
> WILLA CATHER

as much as I loved being there, I'd hoped Taylor would show us something beyond a slick, highly polished performance. I'd hoped she would share more of herself. When she announced, "I first played in Seattle ten years ago and it's great to be back," I longed for her to acknowledge that she had been fifteen years old at the time. *Fifteen!* I wanted her to say how scared she had been, or even that she wasn't allowed to stay up late after the show—I wanted to see the person behind the performer. Even on an elaborate set filled with smoke and mirrors in a packed football stadium, I longed for the highly produced singer to show some vulnerability. That move would have created a rare sense of intimacy.

I wanted that because I teach students how to write about themselves in the first person, and a good writer in T-Swizzle's position would have taken the opportunity to reflect.

Here's an important issue I will address later in the book. Whenever you write (or talk) about the past, there are two characters called "I." There's the person who's telling the story, the writer at the desk—or in this case, the rock star on the stage—and there's the past self whose experience you're recounting. I had hoped that red-lipsticked young woman on stage would reflect on how she had grown and changed in the past decade. What remained of the girl in a sundress and cowboy boots? What does she know now that she didn't then?

In your essay, that's what you have to do: share a bit of yourself with your readers and reflect on the ways you've developed.

The Right Clothes

We all have different outfits for various occasions. Persona can malfunction in an essay the same way wardrobe can.

Surely you've felt embarrassed and awkward when someone else buys you clothes, especially someone who doesn't know you well or who wants you to look a certain way. Or when you have to put on a stiff and formal suit for a wedding or a funeral or church. These clothes may fit, but they don't feel right. They don't feel like you.

We each have our own style. It may seem like no style—the same Carhartt's and a black T-shirt every day—but it's how we dress when we feel most comfortable. When we have to do something out of the ordinary and our usual clothes won't do, we can get twitchy.

When someone writes an essay and uses big words we know they've never spoken aloud, when the sentence structure is stilted, when semicolons prickle the prose in random places, it looks and feels uncomfortable. All we can see are the embarrassing clothes. We cringe a little. We wonder who is under the layers designed to conceal.

Now, I know in your papers for English class you probably do all those things, or at least some of them. Your teachers may even reward your stiffness: they'll forbid your use of contractions (like *they'll*) and may even dock you for writing in the first person. You might have been taught it's better to use fancy Latinate words like *defecate* instead of the good old Anglo-Saxon *shit*. If you're like me, someone who says *shit* all the time, using *defecate* will make you appear like a pompous jerk. Your essay won't sound like you.

Writing in the first person means not only using "I" but deciding which "I" is doing the narrating. What's the right outfit for the task? I suggest you cast off your uncomfortable school clothes and put on whatever makes you feel best and happiest, the you you most enjoy being. That's what will let a college admissions officer—or a future employer or an online date—see you for the awesome person you are.

3

Sex, Drugs, and Palestinian Statehood

FINDING A TOPIC

Believe it or not, I love assignments. When an editor comes to me and says, *We want you to write about blah blah blah*, I whoop and holler.

Yes! I can write about blah blah blah.

But if they say, *Hey, we want you to write for us, whatever you want*, I freeze. I panic. I can't think of one single thing I could write more than two sentences about. If the whole world is fair game—which, often, it is—how can I possibly figure out the "right" topic?

Maybe you've never had this experience. Maybe you've always been given specific assignments by your teachers. You've been asked to write about the causes of the Civil War, or Darwin's theory of evolution, or the color white in *Moby-Dick*. Even if you're not really interested in the topic, too bad—that's the task.

Because I know how hard it is to be told just to write, I have a slew of prompts I give my students, which generally come out of the reading we've done. When we finished dissecting Martin Luther King Jr.'s gorgeous prose, I asked my prisoners to write an essay called "Letter from a Spokane Jail." After we read "My Favorite Teacher," I ask students to write something using that title. Following a discussion of "Who Shot Johnny," we do an exercise in rage on the page.

College applicants have lots of freedom in terms of choosing an essay topic, but to make things easier, the Common Application and many individual colleges provide a list of prompts. Here are some that have been used recently. They change frequently, but not dramatically.

Some students have a background, identity, interest, or talent that is so meaningful they believe their application would be incomplete without it. If this sounds like you, then please share your story.

The lessons we take from failure can be fundamental to later success. Recount an incident or time when you experienced failure. How did it affect you, and what did you learn from the experience?

Reflect on a time when you challenged a belief or idea. What prompted you to act? Would you make the same decision again?

Describe a problem you've solved or a problem you'd like to solve. It can be an intellectual challenge, a research query, an ethical dilemma—anything that is of personal importance, no matter the scale. Explain its significance to you and what steps you took or could be taken to identify a solution.

Discuss an accomplishment or event, formal or informal, that marked your transition from childhood to adulthood within your culture, community, or family.

Okay, go ahead and write.

If only it were that easy. What these prompts have in common—with the exception of the first one, which can be translated to "Who I am"—is that instead of asking for a static portrait, they all require the writer to focus on struggle or change. Not "who I am" but "how I've become who I am." Your job is to find a topic that will allow you to write about struggle or change in your life in a way that sounds like the best, smartest version of yourself. No, it's not easy, but you can do it.

Punchy Is Revealing

When I did college counseling, I first asked clients to write an autobiography. Tell me about yourself in an email, I'd say. Often I'd get back twelve single-spaced pages of delightful, natural prose.

Then I'd ask them to fill out a wacky questionnaire where they had to respond to idiotic questions like "If you were a vegetable, what vegetable would you be?" This allowed me to get to know them a little, to loosen them up, and to see how they write when nothing's at stake. Because as soon as they began to write The College Application Essay, it was as if they'd put on a rented tuxedo: no matter how many times it's been cleaned, it still reeks of the many different people who've worn it. So I had them do a bunch of throwaway writing for my eyes only. And then I showed them how much of what they considered warmups we'd be able to use in the real thing. Usually in that first autobiographical rambling we could find the kernel of a great personal essay.

Then I asked them to list twenty (20!) possible essay topics. They had to get to twenty. The first few were usually easy. And often typical.

1. Basketball = Life.
2. My community service experience in a developing country, where I learned poor people can be happy.
3. I miss my dead grandma.
4. I'm interested in both the sciences and the humanities.
5. Being captain of the debate team.
6. Tennis = Life.

7. My Eagle Scout project.
8. I hate my little brother.
9. I want to save the world.

When they got into the higher numbers, the topics became weird and specific:

10. My second toe is bigger than my big toe.
11. I'm worried about garbage.
12. I eat only beige food.
13. I love popping zits.
14. Cheez-Its are superior to Cheese Nibs.
15. Physics homework makes me want to cry.
16. I keep locking my keys in my car.
17. I'm bad at making numbered lists.
18. I've been cooking since I was three years old.
20. I couldn't get a date to the prom.

We'd look over the list and I'd ask them to write a sentence or two on each of the topics they thought might be most fun to write about. The good ones were usually those at the very end, when they were hurting for ideas and got a little punchy. Punchy is good when it comes to essays. Punchy can be revealing.

Be careful, though. There's a fine line between showing your charming and unique self and letting your freak flag fly. If you try too hard, punchy can come off as annoying and gimmicky. You still have to be honest and authentic. If you're unsure whether you've gone too far, have people read your essay and listen carefully to their comments.

Stay Small and Close

One of my early counseling clients, Tim, wanted to go to New York University. It was his first, and really only, choice.

Given his grades and his test scores—good but not great—I thought it was a long shot.

I asked Tim to write his autobiography. He did. He wrote about his family, his parents' divorce, summer camp, sailing, living in a tourist town in Maine, changing schools, music he loved, LARPing (live action role playing), wanting to make films, being Jewish, being gay, his first boyfriend.

After I read all that, he told me he wanted to write his personal statement about an obscure filmmaker.

"Whoa there," I said. "Every hipster and his brother who wants to go to NYU could write that essay."

Tim's mom is also a writer and has an artist's eye for telling details. She said, "He should write about his ear."

She explained that Tim had been born with a congenital birth defect—one of his ears looked like a deformed nubbin and didn't work. A few years before, his parents had taken him to see a plastic surgeon, who said that Tim could get a prosthetic ear that would look completely normal, though he still wouldn't be able to hear. They planned the surgery and traveled to Los Angeles. And then Tim said no. He realized that his stubby little ear was part of him, part of who he was. Perhaps in the future he would be able get it fixed so he could hear; that would be the surgery he wanted.

When we talked about this, he didn't see why I thought his ear would make for a good essay topic. What was the big deal? At my urging, he wrote about his decision not to have surgery on his stub.

Later, at the reception for first-year students at NYU, the dean of admissions approached Tim to tell him how much he loved the essay about his ear. That's your goal: an essay so good it gets passed around the office and up the chain of command.

As Tim's story shows, often we are not the best judges of what makes us unique or unusual. Writing about the ear was Tim's mom's idea. Interview your parents, friends,

> Everybody walks past a thousand story ideas every day. The good writers are the ones who see five or six of them. Most people don't see any.
>
> ORSON SCOTT CARD

and teachers. Maybe ask them to list twenty weird, quirky things about you. They'll start with the obvious stuff. You're smart. Hardworking. Kind. Funny. You love lacrosse. You're as good at English as you are at calculus. You do community service because you like it, not because it's required. You hate avocados. You talk to your cat all the time. You couldn't get a date to the prom so you held your own Non-Prom.

Again, the good stuff usually comes at the end of the list: a Non-Prom? When you made your list, you may have focused on the first part of that last item—no date—because that was hard and bad. You may have forgotten your own resourceful solution to the problem because it seemed obvious to you: to hold a Non-Prom for all the other kids who didn't have dates. That tells us about who you are.

If you don't have anyone to help brainstorm and you remain ignorant about your own awesomeness, try making a list of all the pages you've liked on Facebook, or the people you follow on social media, or the photos you post on Instagram. Websites you've bookmarked. TV shows you love. You might see some patterns. So many photos of rats! You sure do like the color blue. Sock monkeys! You're all about sock monkeys! You've seen every episode of *Project Runway*. You want a TARDIS.

Look around your room. What do you have a lot of? Do you see one pair of boots and eighteen pairs of running shoes? A zillion pig figurines? Stacks of vinyl records you stole from your dad? Are all your clothes black? Our collections say a lot about us. If you focus on something small and close, you can show the reader something big about yourself.

"Oh No! I Don't Have a Tragedy"

Students often think that if they don't have a good tragic story, if they haven't survived forty-seven days alone on a raft on the Pacific, if they haven't climbed Everest solo without oxygen, if they haven't nearly died from cancer of the funny bone, they're screwed. In fact, it's the opposite. It doesn't matter how exciting or terrible your life has been if you can't write about it in a way that's interesting. Good essayists, like comedians, can find a way to make anything—including nothing—compelling.

Perhaps you've never failed. You're a good kid. You listen to your parents and teachers. Nothing tragic has ever happened to your family, who all get along and take fabulous trips together, and really, your mom *is* your best friend. Then what?

First, take a moment to feel happy and grateful for your good fortune. That's important.

Then, well, you have the whole world left to write about. You can choose anything to serve as a vehicle to let the reader understand who you are as a person, as a thinker, as a student, and as a friend, including, well, vehicles.

Write about whatever keeps you up at night. That might be cars, or coffee. It might be your favorite book. It might be the Pythagorean Theorem. It might be the situation in the Middle East, or why you don't believe in evolution or how you think kale must have hired a PR firm to get people to eat it.

The personal essay has to be personal—it has to be about you—but we can learn a lot about you from what you choose to focus on and how you describe it.

In English class you may have heard your teacher toss around some fancy literary terms. You may even have been asked to memorize them and been quizzed on the definitions of *metonymy*, *alliteration*, and *oxymoron*.

For the purposes of the essay, a useful device you don't have to memorize the name of is the *objective correlative*. This is where you use an object to carry the emotional weight of the topic.

One of my favorite essays from when I worked in admissions at Duke started out, "My car and I are a lot alike." The writer then described a car that smelled like wet dog and went from zero to sixty in—well, it never quite got to sixty.

Another guy wrote about making kimchi with his mom. They'd go into the garage and talk, really talk. "Once my mom said to me in a thick Korean accent, 'Every time you have sex, I want you to make sure and use a condo.' I instantly burst into laughter and said, 'Mom, that could get kind of expensive!'" A girl wrote about her feminist mother's decision to get breast implants.

Your car, kimchi, Mom's boobs—these are objects or vehicles that allow the writer to get at what he or she has come to say. The essays are not about the car, food, or boobs. These objects allow the writer to explore the real subject: *This is who I am and why I'm like this.*

Take Little Bites out of Big Issues

But if you want to write a less personal essay, if you want to tackle a big issue, go right ahead. If your desire is to produce a policy proposal on how to solve the problem of Palestinian statehood, don't let me stand in your way.

Remember the goal: to allow the reader to get to know you. It's not about the facts, not about making an argument that would be appropriate in a debate or in a newspaper editorial. You have to tell us why you care about this problem, why it matters to you. Maybe it's because you went on a birthright trip to Israel and you met a Palestinian boy. Maybe you stayed up all night talking and he told you about his life, how he and his people have been treated on their own land. Maybe his explanations called into question everything you thought you knew, and after a lifetime of believing Israel should take that chunk of land away from the Arabs, you changed your mind and came to think of Palestinian statehood as necessary and morally right.

Or maybe you went with your parents to Israel and stayed on a kibbutz and everyone you talked to either had been to war or was preparing to enter the army. Maybe you thought about your great-great-grandfather, about the numbers tattooed on his forearm, maybe you remembered seeing photos from Auschwitz, grotesque piles of Jewish shoes and teeth. Maybe someone once painted a swastika on the sidewalk in front of your house. Maybe you thought, *Never again. The Jews have to have a homeland.*

People might advise you against taking on a subject like the geopolitics of the Middle East. As with prayer in school, abortion, the legalization of marijuana, and transgender rights, you could easily get yourself into trouble because you're bound to find readers who don't agree with you. If you're applying to a conservative Catholic school, for example, you may not want to produce an essay making fun of the pope. (Though I have the feeling that the current pope enjoys a good joke.) Whenever we write anything, we need to be aware of our audience.

If you really care about an issue—even if it's a hot-button topic—go for it. It's not what you write about; it's how you do it. If you were to create a rant listing all the reasons the Israelis need to get out of Palestine, we might wonder why you think you have the authority to pronounce on a matter that has kept some of the best minds of our world stumped for decades. But if you were to tell us a story that showed your connection to the question, even if we disagreed with you, we'd have a better idea of who you are and what you stand for.

If the situation in the Middle East keeps you awake at night, write about it. But write to figure out what you believe, not to tell us what we should think or do. The essay has to be about you. Remember, your thesis is always "This is who I am." The essay might turn into "I'm an American-born secular Jew who didn't think about international affairs until I went to Israel, where I learned how little I understand about the world." Or "I'm an altar boy who went to Jerusalem with my grandparents, followed the Stations of the Cross, and realized politics and religion have always been mixed together."

You have to write the essay that only you—with your distinct background and values and parents and friends and experiences—can write.

Failure Is Gold

Maybe this doesn't happen to you, but when I succeed—when a book is published, when I run faster than I thought I could in a race—I feel great for about thirty-seven seconds and then I go back to my normal life. When I fail—when I get (another) rejection, when I cross the finish line minutes or even hours after I should have—the disappointment and sadness linger for days and sometimes months. Usually it feels worse to lose than it feels good to win.

From those long moments of sitting with failure we have the opportunity to come back stronger, like bones that have been broken. After I finish licking my wounds and beating myself up, I try to figure out where I went wrong. Had I aimed too high? Did I make a newbie mistake like wearing brand-new shoes in a marathon?

The truth is, we tend not to learn much from our successes. We run a good race and we say to ourselves, *Yay me!* We congratulate ourselves on knowing what to do and then doing it. We discover nothing. But failure? Failure is gold.

Your job, as a writer, is to look at times you've messed up, and the accompanying shame, head on. As soon as you write about the thing you don't want anyone to know, you may feel unburdened. You've written it down and—oh my gosh—you've survived. If you keep writing, you may discover how strong you really are.

In an essay called "Compensation," Ralph Waldo Emerson wrote that when a great man is "pushed, tormented, defeated, he has a chance to learn something; he has been put on his wits, on his manhood; he has gained facts; learns his ignorance; is cured of the insanity of conceit; has got moderation and real skill." (The same is true for women, Uncle Ralphie.)

When we fail, make mistakes, or realize we were wrong, well, that's when we grow. We push against our own limits, and the test becomes not what we've done but how we think. What have we learned? How has it changed us?

Most of us take great delight in being right and hate being wrong. It's hard to forgo the pleasure of a juicy "I told you so." We can be wrong about ideas only in retrospect; we are usually unaware of our mistakes in the present tense, though of course we sometimes make choices that we know—even in the moment—are bad, like eating a whole bag of candy corn or waiting until the last minute to start a twenty-page paper. To me, one of the most interesting questions you can ask someone is *What have you changed your mind about?*

> It ain't whatcha write, it's the way atcha write it.
>
> JACK KEROUAC

Do you have a cautionary item that reminds you of a time you messed up? A book given to you by a boyfriend who turned out to be a jerk. A broken tennis racket from when you got mad after you lost a match. A note your sister wrote when you hurt her feelings. Any of those would be a good vehicle for an essay.

Failure is, after all, an essential part of every hero's journey. Think about the structure of your favorite adventure movies. They tend to all follow the same pattern, one that's as old as *The Odyssey* and holds true for everything from *The Wizard of Oz* to *Star Wars* to *Finding Nemo*. The hero leaves his ordinary world and is called to action. He may try to demur. He may have a mentor or helper who encourages him. He accepts the mission, impossible as it may seem. On the way he is challenged and tested.

And then things fall apart. He gets captured. Stuck. He goes into a cave and sulks. The hero must be able to overcome that dark moment and crawl out of his pain cave in order to reach his full potential. From that time, when everything is bleak, the hero, face down in the arena, rises and eventually triumphs.

Think of your own hero's journey. You really wanted to play baseball. You were afraid to try out for the team. Then your older sister showed you how to pitch. In your first game, you got lit up by every batter you faced. You went to the bench and sat by yourself, head in hands. You wanted to quit. You wanted to cry. You were in your pain cave. As a writer, you will need to stay here. Think about that time. What got you off the bench and back onto the pitcher's mound? It doesn't matter at that point if you strike out every person on the opposing team. What we want to see is what it took—what came from inside you—to get off the bench and jog back onto the field.

My Summer Job, My Great Family, Blah Blah Blah

Of course it's also possible to write about good times, things that you're passionate about, and mundane topics like work and hobbies, but again the key to making these topics work is writing about them in a way that only you can.

You've probably had a job. Maybe it's setting the family table for dinner, or mowing the lawn, or maybe you're a veteran barista and can draw flowers and write poems into the foam of a latte.

Sure, it helps to have had an unusual job or an extraordinary experience, but that's not necessary for a good essay. One of my students wrote about what he learned as a pizza delivery guy. When you knock on people's doors, you get a big (sometimes scary) window into humanity. Another wrote about working in a potato factory. I've read essays about making Subway sandwiches. None of these is a unique job, but each person experiences it differently, and they can write about it in a way that reflects who they are and what they care about.

Many of my favorite essays are about family, something each of us is an expert on, and each of us has stories that only we could tell. But beware of the bland and the generic:

My mother is my favorite person in my life because I can talk to her about everything, she loves me unconditionally and is always supportive.

My mom has taught me to always try my best, to treat everyone equally, to not give up when things get hard.

My mom is my best friend because we share a unique bond that only mothers and daughters can share.

My mom has always been here for me each and every day of my life to instill the values I need to make the best

> of my talents and to make the success that is awaiting me come forth.

You can't argue with any of these statements. But how do they serve to introduce us to the writers? What do we know about the people who would make such statements? Who are these mothers?

If we each wrote an essay about our mom (or dad or sibling or dog), it should be an essay that could come only from us, from our unique experiences and our unique relationship.

Remember my advice to steal from other essayists? Consider how writer Scott Russell Sanders starts his essay "Under the Influence":

> My father drank. He drank as a gut-punched boxer gasps for breath, as a starving dog gobbles food—compulsively, secretly, in pain and trembling. I use the past tense not because he ever quit drinking but because he quit living.

That's some vivid writing. Sanders looks hard at his dad, clear-eyed and unsentimental. You feel his loss by his word choice. He doesn't say that his father died but rather that he "quit living." The action in that word *quit*, as if it were a choice, like walking out on a job or giving up cigarettes, contains the world of a hurt son. The rest of the essay is in the same spirit: a piece only he could write about his dad.

Sarah Vowell's essay "Shooting Dad" starts like this:

> If you were passing by the house where I grew up during my teenage years and it happened to be before Election Day, you wouldn't have needed to come inside to see that it was a house divided. You could have looked at the Democratic campaign poster in the upstairs win-

dow and the Republican one in the downstairs window and seen our home for the Civil War battleground it was. I'm not saying who was the Democrat or who was the Republican—my father or I—but I will tell you that I have never subscribed to *Guns & Ammo*, that I did not plaster the family vehicle with National Rifle Association stickers, and that hunter's orange was never my color.

About the only thing my father and I agree on is the Constitution, though I'm partial to the First Amendment, while he's always favored the Second.

Look at all those vivid details. Vowell goes on, in funny prose, to discuss guns and her relationship with her dad and ends on an unexpectedly poignant note.

Try, Try, and Try Again

After all this, if you're still not sure what to write about, consider that the form of the essay started with a sixteenth-century philosopher, Michel de Montaigne, who took as his motto "What do I know?" and then, by writing, tried to figure it out. His essays were digressive, contained anecdotes and personal ruminations, and ranged among many subjects. Here are some of his essay titles:

Of Idleness
Of Quick or Slow Speech
Of Liars
Of Fear
Of Friendship
Of Moderation
Of Cannibals
Of Sleep
Of War Horses
Of Smells

Of Drunkenness

Of Books

Of Cruelty

Of Thumbs

Of a Monstrous Child

Of Vanity

Of the Custom of Wearing Clothes

Of the Giving of the Lie

Of Three Good Women

Of the Most Excellent Men

Of Cripples

Montaigne used each of these topics as a starting point, but his subject was always himself. Here's how he described his project: "I want to be seen here in my simple, natural, ordinary fashion, without straining or artifice; for it is myself that I portray."

If you're still looking for topics, I've given you more than twenty you could borrow from Uncle Michel. Each of us could write an essay about friendship. Or cruelty. Or vanity. You may not want to write your college application on drunkenness, but I'm sure you could write about idleness or liars. Or thumbs. Who among us doesn't have a lot to say about thumbs?

Write about whatever will allow you to bring the reader into your world and show her who you are and what you care about, and do it in a way that sounds like your best, smartest self.

AMANDA + JIM

One of my early college counseling ~~victims~~ clients was a girl I'll call Amanda. I asked her to list twenty possible topics, and from those I selected a handful and advised her to write a paragraph or so on each one describing what she thought the essay could be about.

Here's what she came up with.

Warning: not everyone's early drafts are this good. Don't feel bad if you read these and think, I can't do that. You can. Just pay attention.

JIM

I fall for the geeks. The skinny, tall, engineering-inclined nobodies with dark hair and blue eyes. They usually do not like to dance and are not interested in girls. But they're smart, they're funny. They're kind of cute, mainly because of personality quirks.

This guy was perhaps the epitome of my description. His name was Jim. An almost annoyingly short, simple word for the past three years of obsession, yearning, and disappointment in my life. I fell for him, and in doing so, lost my sense of self for a while. I am just now truly recovering. He is ubiquitous in my high school experience, having influenced significant aspects of my recent teenage development, both negatively and positively.

Yet I do not regret my prolonged crush. Cross country, my interest in physics, my growing involvement at church, chess, Jim was linked to all of those. And in the end, my interactions with him helped me discover what I am all about, that I don't have to shape myself into what I think guys want me to be, another step toward a strong self-identity. Now, I can move forward in my life, knowing better who I am and who I need to be with.

HOW I PLAY CHESS

I remember my introduction to chess well. I was sitting in my health independent study class freshman year, which happened to be a study hall for everyone else. My teacher was busy, so she suggested that a chess expert in the class teach me how to play the game. I was dressed up as Audrey Hepburn in *Breakfast at Tiffany's*, because it was Celebrity Day of Spirit Week. I carefully slipped off my white glove, and the game began.

As I became accustomed to the rules, plays, and pieces, I developed a strategy, as nearly any chess player does. The more games I played, the more I realized how much my strategy in chess correlated with my "strategy" in life, especially in relationships.

Thankfully, my strategies in both chess and relationships have changed over time. I see now that I cannot control either game, despite my vigorous efforts to do so. Sometimes I win, sometimes I lose, but in the end, I learn, and that's what counts. Always being on defense, passively avoiding trouble, cannot often lead to significant success.

I am now more willing to take chances and grasp opportunities when I get them. I've slipped off my spotless, protective cover and am ready to get dirty. Funny how a common board game has prompted me to reconstruct my entire relational approach.

GEEKY CHEERLEADER

"Intellectual cheerleader." The phrase is practically an oxymoron. Stereotypically, cheerleaders are supposed to be bleach-blonde, tan, skinny, ditzy, mean, popular girls who like bouncing around in short skirts. I was none of those things. I just liked watching basketball games and cheering my guy buddies on. But I tried to fit in to the stereotype, to some extent, in junior high. I attempted to hide my intelligence, wore lots of makeup, and stopped reading outside of school.

Then, in high school, I realized that I was not alone as a cheerleading nerd. My coach was a calculus teacher, and my team captain was valedictorian her senior year. Slowly, I began to realize that I didn't have to fit the personality profile or "the look" to do an activity.

DIETING/CROSS COUNTRY

I have been dieting in one way or another since I was twelve. Even before then, there were certain unhealthy foods that were absolutely never in the house. I would always look forward to slumber parties as opportunities to eat all the yummy junk food I never had the opportunity to indulge in at home.

The way I have dieted in the past few years reflects my extreme personality. It was my own all-or-none phenomenon. I would give up a food or food group, often a combination of several, completely, no excuses. Naturally, I got a lot of attention from this approach; I am still thought of as "the health nut" in my circle of friends. Then, some event or situation might trigger me to eat the food, after months or even years of not having it. After a taste of that food, I would be a goner. I would over-indulge, eating way too much of that food way too often.

During junior high and freshman year, the dieting was just to keep me healthy, not to lose weight. However, it evolved into weight-loss attempts sophomore year, after consuming tons of carbs in cross country. The situation escalated junior year, and I am just now figuring out how to balance my diet, as well as other aspects of my life, effectively.

My struggle with dieting has taught me simply this: it shouldn't be a struggle. I should not let my emotions affect what and when I eat. Eating healthy foods needs to be a decision I make and stick to, regardless of circumstances. I have seen what dieting and bingeing can do to people, how they ironically lose control of their lives by trying to control what their bodies digest. And I have also realized that being an extreme person in general is not healthy. Life is not black and white, and I have to act accordingly.

Which of these topics do you think would make for a good essay? I thought any of them would do, mostly because, as you can see, Amanda is a serious and reflective thinker and a lively writer.

That Amanda put Jim first gave me a hint that she might want to do her essay about him. So I wrote back to her:

This is your essay, because (1) it will allow you to talk about a variety of interests (you could probably squeeze ideas from each of these samples into this one); (2) you will be able to write it with passion, humor, and insight, and (3) there's no way an admissions officer will forget it.

So—of course it's up to you—this is the one I'd like you to work on. Before you sit down to write I want you to spend some time thinking about how you want to structure and craft this essay. Go for a run. Think about how to start it. At the beginning—with how you met him? At the end, when you're trying to get over him? You need to have what we in the creative nonfiction biz call a "narrative arc." Think of the shape of the essay. It has to start somewhere. Then it takes us on a journey, as it were, and ends somewhere else which, at the conclusion of the essay, seems almost inevitable, or at least to make sense. This is very, very hard to do. But you are a sophisticated enough writer and thinker that I want you to do more than think about what kinds of information to include. I want you to think about crafting this as a piece of work.

Don't let yourself start writing right away. I'm not kidding about this. It has to percolate for a while until you can't wait to write it. Then, when you're ready, write it.

I've highlighted some of the things from the other topics that I think are interesting and, if you can, might be nice to shoehorn in here. But you will know what fits and what doesn't.

Amanda found a great structure for the essay itself. She started every paragraph with "Jim was":

Jim was my tutor.
Jim was my type.
Jim was my athletic motivation.
Jim was my engineer.
Jim was my crush.
Jim was my god.
Jim was my madness.
Jim was my secret.

This structure allowed Amanda to show all the ways she had contorted herself to make Jim like her. In the end, she became a great chess player, a better runner, interested in engineering, and closer to her church. She ended with this:

Sure, Jim "broke" my heart. And in pursuit of him, I gave up my identity for a while. But in the end, my heart mended, and my identity returned, stronger, better, and more diverse than before. Plus, in losing Jim, I found activities and ideas I liked even more than him, passions that remained long after my crush was gone.

It was a terrific essay from a good, smart writer. Amanda used Jim as a vehicle to talk about her various and diverse interests.

What's most amazing to me about this is that whenever I talked to Amanda about it afterward, it always made her uncomfortable. At first I thought it was false modesty. No. It turns out that although she was happy with the essay, whenever she thought about Jim she felt like a failure.

When I asked her, a decade after she'd graduated from college, if I could use her material in this book, she said,

"Even now, I'm not completely comfortable thinking about that whole situation. Not like I'm upset now that he didn't like me, but I think of myself then and how upset I was. So many crushes came afterwards, and several before, but I was so hung up on Jim."

Amanda had picked a topic that mattered to her, something that kept her up at night. In the course of writing the essay, she figured out how she had changed and grown even though she never got the boy. It still hurt not to get the boy. That Amanda forced herself to say the hard things gave her essay emotional richness and honesty, and that's what made it so good.

4
Aboutness

AN ESSAY IS OFTEN ABOUT SOMETHING OTHER THAN WHAT IT'S ABOUT

Once you find a topic that really interests you, you'll have to take the next step and figure out what the essay will be about.

What do I mean by that?

Well, every piece of writing has what Vivian Gornick calls a situation and story. The situation is the topic. Maybe it's making the varsity basketball team, or learning how to play the guitar, or your pet boa constrictor. But the story will be what you learned from that experience. It's what I like to call the "aboutness." Rafael the boa constrictor could be the topic, but the essay might be about why you like having a snake—because you're a girl who embraces misunderstood creatures. Or, it may be about how living with a snake has forced you to think about becoming a vegetarian. You love Rafael, but you have to feed him live rats. You get attached to the rats. That makes you question your own eating habits. Can you justify eating meat if you love animals? Is a plant-based diet a reasonable alternative for you, if not for Rafael?

After you land on a topic, you'll need to figure out a problem you'd like to try to solve for yourself. Every essay is an attempt to answer a question. It might be *Why did I want a snake in the first place?* Or *How can I continue to eat meat if feeding my snake makes me sick?* An essay must be more than a list of achievements, more than reporting on an event. What happened matters less than what you learned from the experience—about yourself, other people, or the world.

That's why you and I and twenty-three of our closest friends could go to the state fair together and write twenty-five completely different essays. You might focus on the rodeo because you think bull riders are badass, even though many of them are short. If you're a small guy, this might make you feel better about yourself. Someone else might describe the chicken competition. So many kinds of chickens! Some look like golden retrievers and others resemble bunnies. That person might start thinking about the variety found in nature, then turn her thoughts to people, and end with a meditation on the importance of diversity in schools. I might write about frozen chocolate-covered bananas. Perhaps when I bite into one of those sticks of deliciousness at the fair I recall a family trip to Disney World and understand that was when I first became aware of the trouble in my parents' marriage.

Many students who do "creative writing" produce pages that read like a cheesy novel instead of an essay—a narrative of events, one after the next, often told in a breathless voice, maybe in the present tense, crammed with dialogue, too much scene setting, and sometimes unfortunate attempts at sound effects: *Thwack! Bam!* (I'll explain why these are bad choices in a later chapter.)

From sitting around campfires to reading the epic tales of the ancient Greeks, we tell ourselves—and others—stories in order to live, in order to understand and to be understood. But for the purposes of an essay, you have to do more than that. You have to tell a good tale, and then you have to figure out what it means and why it matters. In other words, it has to be *about* something. It needs an "aboutness."

> Anecdotes don't make good stories. Dig down so far that what finally comes out isn't even what you thought it was about.
>
> ALICE MUNRO

Beginning fiction writers are often admonished, "Show, don't tell." But essayists have to show *and* tell. One of the differences between fiction and nonfiction is that much of the suspense in novels or short stories comes from what your English teacher may have called "dramatic irony," where the reader knows more than the character. It's the "Don't go in the house!" moment in scary movies where the viewer knows there's a dude hiding in a closet wearing a crazy mask and holding a knife, while the protagonist merrily makes himself a pb&j in the kitchen. In novels we often "read around" a character who may be unreliable or unaware. We'll see what he's missed or how she's lied to herself. Part of the pleasure of fiction comes from watching characters learn and grow.

In a personal essay, the writer has to know more than the reader. Always. As I've said, in each essay about a past event there are two characters named "I": the writer at the desk—the "I" who is telling the story—and the "I" of the time of the past events. The writer at the desk gets to observe the previous version of herself—with forgiveness, compassion, and grace—and reflect on what she knows now that she didn't back then. This is why, as I'll explain later, the present tense rarely works for personal essays about past events.

We have to be in control of our personas—both of them, the writer at the desk and the younger self—and when we tell a story, it's on us to figure out why the topics we choose are important and what they mean. An essay has to go beyond merely reporting or describing. It has to be about something other than what it's about.

Great essays often use a trivial event to tell us about something big. E. B. White's essay "Once More to the Lake" is ostensibly about returning to the place he spent his summers as a boy, but it's really about mortality and awareness of the inevitability of death. John McPhee uses an imaginary game of Monopoly to write about urban decay in Atlantic City in "The Search for Marvin Gardens." In Chuck Klosterman's book *I Wear the Black Hat*, an essay called "Hating the Eagles" catalogs all the bands he disdained in his younger years, including Coldplay: "I wrote a book in 2001 where I claim, 'Coldplay is absolutely the shittiest fucking band I've ever heard in my entire fucking life.' This is possibly the most memorable thing I've ever written and arguably the stupidest." The essay is about growing up and learning to change his mind. (Many of my students adore Klosterman's essay collection *Sex, Drugs, and Cocoa Puffs*.)

A bad move is to write explicitly about an emotion—the sadness you felt when your goldfish died, how much you hate physics, your love of music. If those are the feelings you want to explore, find an object or an event that will serve as a vehicle to talk about the emotion. Let an empty fishbowl stand in for your grief. Describe how vectors became your nemesis. Write about your guitar as if it were a friend.

The best essays stay small and close. They use something trivial (a 3-4-5 triangle, making dinner, a car) to open out into something big (a love of math, a connection to family, who you are).

Tell a Story, Have Some Thoughts

Now I'm going to give you the best advice I've ever heard about how to write an essay. Ready?

Tell a story. Then have some thoughts.

It's that simple. Good essays do this repeatedly. They layer narrative (the situation or the event) and reflection (thoughts that dig into the aboutness). If you go back and look at the carefully constructed prompts offered by the Common App folks, you'll see that's what they're looking for. Each prompt contains a two-part assignment. You're asked to recount an incident, describe a problem, or discuss an accomplishment or event, and then you're asked to figure out what it meant to you.

Now that may seem simple, but it's not. The aboutness can be the thing that's hardest to get to, the part where, if you press too hard, it hurts. We tend to avoid discomfort by writing around the central issue—what I call the hole in the donut (which I'll discuss in the next chapter). We'd rather write about our achievements, because it feels better than exposing our weaknesses and vulnerabilities. But if you're writing around something, the reader will wonder what you're hiding. She'll see that you're not giving her the whole scoop, which is usually messy and complicated.

So how do you get there?

Okay, I'll walk you through it.

First, open a new document. At the top of the page, copy and paste the prompt you're planning to use. Let's use this one from the Common App:

```
Discuss an accomplishment or event, formal or infor-
   mal, that marked your transition from childhood to
   adulthood within your culture, community, or family.
```

Now, though you will later go back and edit it out, type, "The event that first made me feel like a grownup was _____," and see what happens. I say you will edit it out because only the lamest and most ham-handed essays restate the prompt. But we won't worry about that now. The time for elegance comes later. At this point you want to see what you say about that this event. Don't forget that: we write to find out what we think. You may get to a place that surprises you.

Write everything you can remember about that situation. Tell a story. Take us through the day. Be specific and vivid. Add details. Avoid generalizations. But don't edit yourself. Don't try to make it perfect. Just get it all down on the page. Write and write and write. Have fun as you remember. Go ahead, brag.

And then add some thoughts.

How do you do that? Each time you write a declarative sentence ("When I aced my driver's license test, I felt free"), follow it by writing, "By that I mean ____," and see what you say. It might be something like "I hadn't realized how hobbled I felt always having to ask my older sister for rides, how relying on my friends meant I sometimes stayed later at parties than I wanted to, how I could never go anywhere by myself."

Then look at what you've come up with and pull each phrase apart. Why did you hate asking your sister for rides? You might write, "I hated asking my sister for rides because she was a witch and made fun of me when I wanted to go to the park to feed the squirrels." Why does that matter? "That matters because even though I know they're wild animals and should be able to find their own food, I think it's nice for squirrels to have meals delivered."

Later you might decide nothing about your sister or the

> There is no story that is just one story. Every story is two stories. It is the one on the surface, and the one bubbling beneath.
>
> GRACE PALEY

squirrels is interesting. But keep going. Look at the phrase "I wanted to be able to drive places by myself because," and then wonder, *Hey, what's that about? Why did I want to go by myself?* You're a social person. You have lots of friends and come from a big family. But being able to drive into the country, surrounded by fields and grazing cows, appeals to you. What is that about? Why might that make you feel like a grownup?

Maybe it has to do with realizing you're different from your siblings. Instead of wanting to go to college and then move to New York City the way they all did, you can imagine yourself riding a horse on the plains. Even though you've never been farther west than Chicago, you might add, "The image of the West appeals to me because," and who knows where that will lead. Maybe you first felt like an adult when you realized you wanted to leave the East Coast, where you'd spent your whole life, and move to a different part of the country because you saw photos of Yellowstone, or you read a lot of John Muir's work, or maybe you love John Wayne movies and see yourself as a loner hero type.

This is the process of going deeper. Each time you make a statement, ask yourself, *Why do I think that?* And then type, "I think that because ____." Write that exact phrase, even though it feels clunky. I learned this trick from a poet who, when she gets stuck on a poem and wants to plumb deeper, adds all sorts of "By that I mean" statements that get her to think harder. Then she goes back and deletes them all. What's left is the good stuff.

Writers sometimes refer to these kinds of props as "scaffolding," like the temporary structures that help in building houses. When the project is finished, the scaffolding goes away, but you couldn't have done without it during the construction stage.

Now you've written yourself a long way from the driver's test. You may in fact have pounded out twelve single-spaced pages. Sweet! I'll discuss the tasks of cutting and revision in later chapters, but here's a preview: good writers enjoy editing and know that you have to murder your darlings—take out the pieces that you love but that don't belong in the essay—in order to write well. You may have to get rid of some hilarious remarks about your witchy sister, or a detailed recap of your career in food service for squirrels. Save these. You may find a use for them in another essay.

But your work isn't done. You also have to show growth, which often comes from conflict. And that's something most of us would prefer not to write about. Even once we've landed on a good topic, and we've figured out the aboutness, in early drafts we write around the parts that are most painful.

Your job is to go there.

ADAM FINDS HIS PIRATES

I once worked with a kid named Adam who had an experience that shaped him in profound ways. He'd been selected through a competitive process to attend the last remaining caddy camp in the United States.

Caddy camp? That's where you learn how to be a golf caddy. Apparently this place, on the New England island of Nantucket, attracts some of the wealthiest and most powerful people in the world. Each summer sixty boys are selected to learn how to caddy for them.

No question—a cool experience, and one that meant a lot to Adam. He kept writing about how great it was. He dropped the names of famous people whose golf clubs he had lugged around. He talked about how privileged he felt to have been selected to participate. A wonderful opportunity, but that didn't make for a strong essay.

Adam wrote vague and general sentences including "I was on a journey full of mystery and opportunity, where I could explore a new land and embark on a path full of wonder, hard work, leadership, commitment, teamwork, and success." We've all written a sentence or two like that; the problem is it could be about getting a new puppy or auditioning for *Naked and Afraid*.

As we went through draft after draft, Adam's descriptions got more vivid and specific and I started to get a sense of being at camp. But I still didn't see what Adam had learned other than caddying. How had he changed? He was reluctant to complain or appear critical. It was all puppies and rainbows and lollipops. So I pushed him.

On each draft I'd add phrases like "I later realized ____" or "Then I discovered ____" or "It occurred to me that ____." He was missing reflection. He described the place, which is good, and started to tell a story, which is great, but he didn't layer in any thoughts. We saw only the camp, and not the camper. Descriptive writing can put us in a place, but it has to serve a bigger purpose.

Another problem: nothing happened in the essay. Adam's summer job seemed to be completely without struggle. I reminded him of the Common App prompts and pointed out how they were designed to encourage students to go to conflict. *Recount a time when you failed. Write about something that challenged your beliefs. A problem you had to solve. A transition.* The Adam at the start of these drafts—a good kid, a hard worker—was exactly the same as the Adam at the end, except that he'd gotten to hang out on a fancy golf course with a bunch of rich dudes. I didn't learn anything about him or understand what made the experience meaningful and not simply fun.

We went on like this for many revisions. I failed to get Adam to see what was missing. He was eager to do whatever I suggested, but I hadn't asked the right questions.

Finally, we chatted on the phone. I asked him to tell me about a book or movie he loved.

He said, *Captain Phillips*.

I asked Adam to describe the movie. He said Tom Hanks played the captain of a ship taken over by pirates.

That was all I needed to hear. I could figure out the rest. I said, "Okay. He's going along, doing his job, and then pirates come and everything goes to hell and he has to figure out how to save his men."

Adam said, "Well, basically."

Perfect. It's a classic example of the hero's journey.

What I said next to Adam clarified things for him. "Who are your pirates?"

Surely, even at caddy camp, there had to be pirates. Maybe an impatient businessman who yelled at boys for not cleaning the balls fast enough. Maybe counselors who scarfed up all the cookies before the younger kids got to them. Most likely, I suspected, the pirates came in the form of other campers.

Sure enough, the kid who slept in the bunk above Adam turned out to be his pirate. The guy was, Adam said, his polar opposite, and a source of friction.

Conflict!

So I made Adam tell me all about his bunkmate and the shame he had brought to their corner of the hut. The next draft of his essay started:

Our section was the dirtiest in camp: shoes scattered, clothes spread, candy wrappers tossed, and golf tees and ball markers pressed against the grit of the cement floor. Being a neat-freak and OCD candidate, I consistently nagged my bunkmate, the worst first-year camper, to stay clean, organize his clothes, sweep the floor, and throw away his Starburst and Airhead scraps.

Here we have the beginning of a good essay with lots of specific details about two characters who we know will be in conflict: the slovenly bunkmate and the writer who wants to run a tight ship. How did they work out their differences? What did Adam learn in the process?

Good essays need pirates. They may come in less dramatic forms than a bunch of Somali swashbucklers. You're going about your life (on a boat, at a new school, taking a trip to Mexico). You feel uneasy. Something happens that changes the situation (pirates, a racist teacher, a letter from home). You face the challenge and come out the other side stronger for it. You learn. You grow.

Find your pirates.

Then tell a story and have some thoughts.

It sounds easy. It isn't. Especially when you're writing about stuff you'd prefer not to dwell on, like your own mistakes. Adam had to face the ways in which *he* was not a perfect bunkmate. Even after he'd found his pirates, Adam had to keep digging until he hit the hard part, the ways *he* had failed. In other words, he had to stop writing around the hole in the donut.

5

The Hole in the Donut

SAYING THE HARDEST THING

Writing an excellent personal essay can require you to perform uncomfortable emotional archaeology. You have to search for that well-hidden part of yourself, something you might wish weren't there. Once you find it, you have to bring it out into the open, dust it off, and look—really look—at it. The best writers dig in and then keep excavating in the muck because they know that's where the treasures are hidden.

Because most of us would prefer to avoid that kind of self-scrutiny, we often write around the most important issue instead of actually tackling it. This is what I call the Hole in the Donut problem.

Many essays try to show the writer as a superhero—and nothing's worse than a braggy document that tells us how great a person the writer is. "I am a resounding leader." "People like to see my smiling face." "I will contribute to your campus in myriad ways." Ick.

One of the questions I've learned to ask myself when reading essays and trying to figure out what's not working well in them is to wonder, *What is this writer afraid of?* When someone brags on the page, my answer to that question tends to be *You feel inadequate*. When someone uses big words they don't actually know, I think, *You're wor-*

> The secret of good writing is telling the truth.
>
> GORDON LISH

ried you're not smart enough. When I read academic papers laden with jargon, I think, *You feel like an impostor.*

A good essayist will show her own weaknesses. It's like having the confidence to go out without makeup. She might be afraid the barefaced version will cause us to judge her—to find her less beautiful, less formidable. She might fear we won't like her anymore. She will be wrong. Once she reveals to us who she is, once we see that the popular pretty girl gets zits too, we will love her and be on her side.

This is counterintuitive for most of us. When we're faced with a high-stakes writing assignment like crafting a college essay, we think we have to give it everything we've got to prove we're worthy. We're tempted to list all of our achievements and make our lives seem as rosy as an English garden. Maybe, because we know most people don't like boasting, we'll attempt a "humble brag": "I'm so lucky, I don't know how this possibly could have happened and I know I don't deserve it, but I've been named Queen of the Six-Toed Cats Who Like to Wear Hats."

A high-achieving medical school applicant once told me she had figured out the "right" answer to the question "What is your biggest flaw?" She beamed with pride as she explained the way to handle that classic job interview query is to say, "I'm a perfectionist." You can probably see why she was so pleased with herself: It's a flaw that's not really a flaw. A humble brag. An obnoxious answer.

But even this topic can make for an effective essay if handled correctly. One of my graduate students wrote an essay about her perfectionism. She said she'd read about well-adjusted perfectionists and those who were maladapted. Unfortunately, she fell into the latter category. In her attempt to perform as well as she could, she often missed deadlines or was so disappointed with her own efforts that she failed to hand in her work. Instead of trying to admit to something no one would ever think of as a real flaw, she showed how this trait had nearly kept her from graduating from college.

Her essay worked because she knew the "right" answer and avoided it. Instead she went to the place that was hard for her to write about—the ways she had failed to be a good perfectionist. That made for a much better essay.

The hole in the donut is the thing you don't want anyone else to see. Maybe it's a mistake you've made, like dropping the game-losing ball. Maybe it's being rejected by someone you really liked. Maybe it's having been a bully. Most of us would prefer not to parade our weaknesses, but we know—and often so does the reader—they're there.

Let me give you two examples.

Mocha Miss

One of my creative writing students submitted an essay about her first horse, Mocha Miss. Breanna had always wanted a horse, and when she was eleven, her parents got her one. Mocha Miss was, she wrote, "quite a handful." She described her challenges with the horse and gave us, right in the beginning of the essay, what felt like a thesis statement: "She taught me to never give up, even when it seems all hope is lost."

When we discussed the piece in class, most of the other students were confused. They didn't understand the horse lingo and didn't see the point of the essay. One of the students summed it up this way: "She gets a horse, the horse was difficult, the horse dies." A characterization perhaps ungenerous but not incorrect. Here's how Breanna ended the essay: "Without [Mocha Miss], I probably would have never joined 4-H, become rodeo royalty, nor be the person I am today." That's fine. It's probably even true. But as readers, we had a hard time caring about either the writer or the horse. We didn't see enough of them to get invested.

Breanna had done what many of us do: she sugarcoated her experience. The horse was clearly a holy terror. I told the class if I were to write this essay, the first sentence might have been "Mocha Miss was an asshole."

Breanna, I knew, would never call anyone, horse or human, an asshole, but she nodded vigorously when I offered my opening line. She agreed that Mocha Miss was the brat I had sensed from the essay, even though we never saw any of their struggles. The essay just reported that the horse had challenged and frustrated the girl. Breanna, the writer remembering the horse ten years later, excused all the mare's bad behavior. She loved Mocha Miss. Mocha Miss was misunderstood. She may not have been an asshole, but she sure was a pain in the neck.

We know Breanna was upset when the horse died. She wrote that it was "one of the worst days of my life" and that she would spare us the "horrible, gross, raunchy details of everything you have to do to try and save a horse from colic, mostly because it is still too hard for me to think about the pain she went through."

Breanna had chosen a topic she really wanted to write about, but she hadn't figured out why it mattered or in

> If you do not tell the truth about yourself you cannot tell it about other people.
>
> VIRGINIA WOOLF

what way. "I loved my horse and was sad when she died" isn't a complicated enough idea to support an essay.

Some members of the class were frustrated because the essay made them feel stupid—they didn't know about horses, and Breanna knew so much that she didn't realize what others might not understand.

Readers do not like to feel stupid. We like to feel smart. We love to acquire new knowledge. At one point in the essay Breanna wrote about when Mocha Miss learned to pick up the correct lead, and then she clarified what that meant—"the front leg that extends first at a lope/gallop." Yes! Never underestimate the power of a good, clear explanation. The trick is to do it in a way that those who are ignorant will feel happily brought out of the fog, and those who are expert will appreciate the explanation and nod in agreement. Breanna's description of leads succeeded in this.

So she had some nice bits, but the essay lacked tension. We wanted to see Breanna as a little kid who got so mad at Mocha Miss she threw a chunk of horse poop at her, and then, later, brought her a carrot and snuggled with her in the barn. She didn't have to tell us she was sorry for getting pissed off at Mocha Miss. If she showed us the scene, we'd know it.

Breanna hadn't made herself say the hardest thing. Like many good kids, she never wanted to badmouth anyone, including a horse she loved. And like most of us, she was reluctant to confess what she felt guilty about. So she wrote a dull and flat essay. Who could argue with "I loved my horse"?

So I asked her, "Where's the conflict here? Is there anything you feel bad about, anything you didn't want to write?"

From across the room I could see Breanna's eyes fill with tears.

She knew exactly the part she didn't want to write, knew

what she wanted to avoid. She knew where to find the pain, the shame.

She said, in a small, trembling voice, "I wasn't there."

Ah. The hole in her donut. In the essay she had written around the issue instead of dealing with it directly. We readers sensed something was missing.

She didn't elaborate, but she didn't need to. We'd found the source of her shame, the reason this topic kept her up at night. That's where the essay needed to get to.

Breanna, the Rodeo Queen, seemed afraid of appearing in the arena without her makeup and curled hair. She didn't want to get into the muck of the hard, sad, uncrowd-pleasing feeling that had driven her to write the essay in the first place. She needed to understand that if she showed herself sitting in an empty stall with mud on her face, we would cry with her. We'd feel her pain.

When a writer asks for sympathy—or worse, pity—we tend to withhold it. When she presents her struggles as facts, when she doesn't try to excuse or airbrush them, we open our hearts. When she says the thing that's hardest to admit, when she goes toward her shame rather than trying to cover it up, we find her courageous and don't judge. We want writers to go to the shame—the things we all feel but most of us are not brave enough to say. And we don't want a simplistic explanation. We want both/and rather than either/or.

Sweaty Miranda

Another student in that college course, Miranda, wrote a funny essay about her hyperactive sweat glands. She grew up in sweltering Las Vegas, and her abundantly perspiring underarms caused her such embarrassment she'd wear oversized sweatshirts in the desert's summer heat to hide her wet spots.

> Confront the dark parts of yourself, and work to banish them with illumination and forgiveness. Your willingness to wrestle with your demons will cause your angels to sing.
>
> AUGUST WILSON

She wrote that while her always-wet palms were annoying—when she tried to do downward dog in yoga, she slid off the mat—her dripping caused a bigger problem for someone else: "My sweating wasn't ideal for my mother or her image—she simply could not be known as the woman whose daughter always had pit stains." In the essay Miranda briefly introduced us to Las Vegas as a place "still stuck in the mindset of 'everything is better when it's plastic.' This is relevant to both credit cards and tits."

Miranda recounted how her mom had pointed to a woman in her twenties and said, "'Oh my gosh, that lady is really pretty! She would look so much better with a nose job, though.' Everything that is seemingly 'broken' may be fixed through a trip to the doctor."

While the bulk of the essay consisted of a detailed description of Miranda's sweat, it soon became clear to those of us in class that the hole in Miranda's donut was her mom, her mom's ideas about beauty, and Miranda's struggle both to live up to them and to reject them. That's a great topic for an essay. And sweaty pits were a good way to get there.

What was Miranda afraid of? Well, duh. No one wants to talk trash about her mom. That's understandable. But no one wants to read an essay that goes on and on: "I love my mom, my mom loves me, it's all good. Puppies! Lollipops! Rainbows!" Miranda needed to describe her mother without blaming her, to portray her as a complex character.

Miranda couldn't be the hero and make her mother into the Wicked Witch of the West.

Miranda's aboutness was that she loved her mom *and* found her values superficial. Breanna's was that she had a difficult horse *and* felt guilty for not being there when the horse got sick. Both/and is always more interesting than either/or.

Most of us have giant long lists of fears that haunt us. We try to keep them hidden, even from ourselves. But if we want to write honestly—and, by the way, to live rich, authentic lives—we need to face these fears. Writing can be therapeutic. If you're angry with someone, it can be helpful to write out your rage. Ask yourself, *What am I most afraid to admit?* And then write about it.

Figure what the hole in your donut is, and then be brave enough to fill it.

> Take your broken heart and make it into art.
>
> CARRIE FISHER

6

Tell Us About Your World in Two Hundred Words

THE SHORT ANSWERS

When I worked in admissions at Duke, sometimes I'd swoon over a terrific long essay and then read the short answers on the Common App supplement with shock and horror. The personal statement would be well crafted and delightful, while the shorties would be full of misspellings and clichés. That discrepancy told me a lot about the applicant and made me wonder whose fingerprints were all over the good essay. You don't want an admissions officer to question your work ethic—or your integrity. Take the short-answer questions as seriously as you do every other part of the application.

The essay prompts vary greatly from college to college. They require responses anywhere from forty to five hundred words. Some ask for a description of an important activity, while others are quirky enough that you won't be able to recycle ("What one invention would you uninvent if you could?"; "What is square one, and can you actually go back to it?" "Describe your favorite 'Bazinga' moment"). Some ask you to write about the books, music, or movies that have been important to you. They'll inquire about what inspires or excites you, and they may also try to solicit information about how you will contribute to diversity on campus.

Colleges use the essay in various ways. Some—like the

University of California system—have even replaced the long essay with several short-answer questions. They seek details about your home environment in order to know how you have taken advantage of the educational opportunities available. You might be asked, "Tell us about your world."

You may not know what is noteworthy or relevant about where you come from. It might seem typical to speak one language at home and another at school. You may believe everyone works fifty hours a week mopping the floor of a nail salon and then stays up until 3:00 a.m. doing homework. If that's what you do, you might not think anything of it. It's normal for you to come home from school and take care of your younger siblings because your mom is at work and if you don't make dinner, they won't eat. Not even worth talking about. (Wrong.)

If you don't know what's unusual about your circumstances, you may want to look to someone outside your immediate community for help, perhaps a relative who lives in another state. Ask a teacher, or a guidance counselor, who isn't a local to describe your community.

Kids from Montana might believe everyone knows what "brain tanning" is. (I learned about it from an applicant to Duke who described using a deer's brain to tan its hide.) Kids from cities might assume most people take the subway to school. Kids from farms might find it odd to learn that not everyone gets up before the sun rises. About sixty-five thousand undocumented immigrants graduate from US high schools each year. Their experiences are vastly different from those of kids who attend suburban prep schools. The essay is the place to think hard about what makes you dissimilar from the larger pool, even if you think you're completely typical in your home community. (You're not.) Where you come from is an important part of who you are.

Grandmas on the Rez

One summer I got to teach a course on the personal essay to Upward Bound students from central Washington. Upward Bound, a federally funded program, helps high school students from low-income families—and from families where neither parent holds a bachelor's degree—get to college.

I brought my dog, Helen, to class, and each day we sat outside for lunch and the kids told me what it was like to be them. Many lived on reservations and were either Native American or the children of Hispanic farmworkers. This group comprised some of the most motivated—and fun—teens I've ever met. They loved music and sports, their pets and their families. They made me laugh, made me think, and paid lots of attention to Helen, who adored them.

These new friends had, I knew, plenty of drama in their lives. They mentioned family members who had died, parents who left them, older sisters who dropped out of high school because they got pregnant, and uncles sent to jail. They didn't mind talking about their struggles.

When it came to working on their application essays, however, my students—whose lives were hard by any measure—refused to recount what they called sob stories. They wanted to write about baseball and their grandmas. That, I told them, was a mistake.

The fact is, these smart, high-achieving students are what many schools are looking for. A key part of a university's mission—especially public schools—is to be inclusive. Most colleges and universities want a diverse and representative student population. Their admissions staff pays attention to the profiles of the high schools from which applicants come. They get census data on the socioeconomic conditions of their communities. They look at family size and income. Does fewer than half the graduating class go on to university? Is the nearest shopping mall three hours away? First-generation college students face different challenges from those whose family names are chiseled onto campus buildings. These facts make a difference in terms of how applications are read.

Colleges want wealthy kids whose families can pay full tuition and fatten their endowments with big donations, and they also want to provide access for those who have been less fortunate. I knew my Upward Bound students would be appealing applicants, but they were reluctant to write about the issues that would show how much they'd had to overcome to get to where they were. These were normal, happy kids, and they didn't see why they should mention their hardships.

Here's the thing. Being a normal, happy kid who loves where he lives, plays music and baseball, and misses his grandma is wonderful. But it won't help the admissions folks who want to lobby to admit you. Your job is to give them ammunition to fight on your behalf, to show how you will contribute to the campus, even if it means writing about "family drama." Help them make the argument. I tried to teach my students both/and. You love baseball, and your family can't afford a new mitt. Your uncle is your role model, and he made mistakes that landed him in prison. Schools don't admit low-income applicants because they're poor; they admit them because these kids have found ways to succeed under challenging circumstances.

Poor Little Rich Kids

Privileged applicants sometimes believe they need to tell tales of woe so it will look like they have overcome adversity. No. For the short-answer questions, as for the long personal statement, your job is to show yourself as honestly, and as fully, as you can. If you were able to earn a pilot's license, or go scuba diving every winter in Fiji, or spend

> Not that the story need be long, but it will take a long while to make it short.
>
> HENRY DAVID THOREAU

spring break at your family's cattle ranch in Argentina, that's great. But be aware that you risk coming off as entitled, at least to some readers.

Like me. When I started working in admissions at Duke, I had little sympathy for applicants whose achievements seemed to come more from their family's checking account than from anything they accomplished on their own. It pissed me off when they were admitted over my objections, often due to the work of people in the alumni or development office.

But when I got to know some of these kids, I learned how they, too, had struggled. Though I had disliked their applications, I overcame my assumptions and grew to adore many kids whose monthly allowance was more than my salary. They had to deal with their own real fears and insecurities, and talked to me honestly about the difficulties of growing up wealthy. They told me stuff I would never have guessed from reading their professionally polished applications. I loved being wrong about them and wished they had gotten better advice when it came to their essays.

Most of my college counseling clients after I left Duke were kids whose parents were able to pay me handsomely. I coached them to acknowledge their privilege and pointed out when they were blind to the uniqueness of their circumstances. "Tell us about your world" is a sincere request, not a judgment. Your task is to try to see how it may appear to an outsider.

Why Us?

Many colleges use the shorties to ask a version of "Why us?" When I was an admissions officer I argued we should get rid of the "Why Duke?" question because 97 percent of the responses were exactly the same and could be boiled down to "great academics, winning sports teams, beautiful campus, good food, nice weather."

The dean of admissions would agree with me and then say, "Yeah, but the 3 percent that do something different are useful." His job was to keep an eye on the big picture, and he was good at his job.

Many smaller colleges track your interest in them. They care whether you've visited, interviewed, emailed questions. They want to admit students who are likely to matriculate. The "Why us?" question allows applicants to show that they're serious about attending and not just trying to rack up acceptance letters.

How do you respond so that the exhausted folks who read thousands of the same *great academics, winning sports teams, beautiful campus, good food, nice weather* answers don't want to stick forks in their own eyes? The truth is a good place to start.

When I was little, we took a family trip to New England and my father declared that I would go to Bennington College and my brother Mark would attend Bowdoin. I have no idea what he based that on, but since I turned into a teenage rebel without a cause, I didn't even apply to Bennington. My brother, however, graduated from Bowdoin, which he loved.

The real reason I wanted to go to Yale was because the summer after my junior year, I went on a program to help rebuild a historic chateau in the Loire region of France. That may sound glamorous, but basically we just hauled around dusty rocks during the day and danced to ABBA in the kitchen at night. However, on that trip were two guys from the same university. They were the most intimidating, arrogant, well-read, scary-smart people I'd ever met. I wanted to be just like them.

Honestly, that's why I wanted to go to Yale.

When I taught at the University of Montana, I had a kid in my first-year composition class named James Gamble Rogers IV. As a former tour guide, I was well aware that James Gamble Rogers had designed much of the architecture at Yale. I found out that my student, Jamie, had been an excellent student at one of the best boarding schools in the country. When I asked him why he came to Montana, he said, "Because I didn't want to go to Yale." Jamie had made his college choice carefully: he wanted to fly fish and study poetry with Robert Pack. He did research, knew what he wanted, and was able to articulate it and easily land a spot in the honors college.

Lots of kids apply to schools they know zip about, except that the name looks impressive on a T-shirt. Many make the decision based on distance from home—either near or far. Some follow older siblings or the paths their parents and grandparents have already trod. Some, like many of my college students, are the first in their family to go beyond high school.

How can anyone be expected to know why they want to go to a place they may never have visited? And how can they write an essay of two hundred words explaining those reasons? What if you don't know why you want to attend each particular college you're applying to? What if you don't know much more about it than the name?

This is an opportunity to do some thinking and, as is always the case for essays, to allow the reader to get to know you. How did you come up with your list of schools? Having grown up in a landlocked state in the middle of the country, are you eager to see what life on the coast—either coast—is like? Did an older student you worshiped attend the college you're applying to, so it's cool by association? Do you love March Madness and so came up with a college list based on your bracket picks? There are no wrong answer. Be honest. Be yourself.

What Do You Plan to Study?

I'm pretty sure that the most popular major for incoming college students is Undecided. Frankly, I think that's great. You may not realize, until you set foot on campus and start taking classes, that you love classical philology. Or ethnobotany. Or molecular biochemistry. But college applications will ask what you want to study, and that may guide where you apply.

Perhaps you're interested in becoming a dog chiropractor. Or a geotechnical engineer. Or a forensic accountant. Taking the time to study each school's viewbook and website can help you figure out what you want to learn and where you might best do that. Just remember that there are many fields you haven't yet heard of that may light you up.

To do a good job with the short essay questions, think about what the most common answer might be and then don't give it. Or if you do, make sure no one else would have responded in the same way.

> The truth is, writing is this: hard and boring and occasionally great but usually not. . . . I have told people that writing this book has been like brushing dirt away from a fossil. What a load of shit. It has been like hacking away at a freezer with a screwdriver.
>
> AMY POEHLER

For example, in my unscientific assessment, 87.4 percent of future engineers respond to the "Why engineering?" question with a one-word answer: Legos.

But what if all those hours of playing with Legos are the real reason you want to learn how to build bridges? Can you make that work?

Of course you can.

Remember that all good writing is vivid and specific.

If you're that kid who spent all of her time building stuff, surely you remember what you built. Maybe you made a giant town out of Legos. You invented stories to go along with each structure, and the people and animals who lived there. And then your cat, Chickenbutt, came in and, like a hurricane, decimated the place. You wanted to flush Chickenbutt down the toilet. But maybe that's when you realized, *Hey, I could do this for real.*

In other words, follow the advice I gave you about the long essay. Write an essay only you could have written—your structures, your stories, your Chickenbutt. Except, with the shorties, you have very little space to do this.

Writing Short

When students complain about having to write a twenty-page paper, I want to say, "You think it's hard for you? Pity your poor teacher!" It is easy to write long. Rambling requires little discipline on the part of the writer and demands much patience from the reader. One of my all-time favorite quotes is from Blaise Pascal: "I would have written you a shorter letter but I didn't have the time."

In a good piece of writing, every word, every sentence, every image has to do work to earn its keep. If you want some examples, read poetry. There's no room for filler in a poem, at least not in a good one. In fact, you should probably take a break right now and read some poetry.

Or look at some of the six-word stories that make the rounds on the internet, the most famous of which is by Ernest Hemingway. Here it is. The whole thing.

```
For sale: baby shoes, never worn.
```

This may have been the start of the form known as flash fiction: Tiny pieces that tell whole stories in as few as six words.

Make no mistake. These are very hard to write well. Learning how to craft short, pithy pieces will help you when you have to apply for jobs, fill out profiles, and ask your parents for money. It's also a skill you'll need to complete the short-answer essays on the college application.

You might be tempted to look at those prompts and think, *Hey, two hundred words! I can crank that out in five minutes.*

Nope. You're basically being asked to write a poem. You'll need to cut out anything that isn't absolutely essential (for example, in this sentence, that would be words like *out* and *absolutely*) and also say something that doesn't sound like it could have been written by any other applicant.

When it comes to writing short, your best strategy may be simply to describe in a direct manner who you are and where you come from. The aboutness is straightforward. "I am a kid who can't leave unwashed dishes in the sink, whose skateboard has more miles on it than many cars, and who prefers to sleep until noon. I want to go to college to study finance because I've seen my mom passed over for promotions since she does not have a degree." Or "Everyone in my family has gone to Cornell. I am not a follower; I like to make my own way. I was not going to apply to Cornell until I met Professor Smith at Comicon in San Diego. She helped me understand that my experience at Cornell can be whatever I make of it—I can blaze my own trail there. I can study with her and do my senior thesis on Wonder Woman instead of being pre-law."

The short answers are important. Treat each blank space on an application as an opportunity to reveal more of what's unique and compelling about you and use the techniques I've been teaching you. Remember to anticipate what a typical response might be and go beyond. When colleges claim that their aim is to get to know you, they're serious. Give them what they need to do this.

EMMA'S SHORTIES

Emma was an anxious sophomore who wrote to me after she read my young adult novel *On the Road to Find Out*. In a heartfelt email, she told me about her life and how her struggles were similar to those of the main character in my book, a girl who takes up running after getting dinged from her first-choice college.

I wrote back right away and we became friends. When it was time for Emma to begin her college application process, I was happy to help out. She'd been recruited to a university for field hockey and got stuck on a short (100-word) essay prompt that went like this:

> Expertise in and experience with imagination, inventiveness and resourcefulness: Illustrate to us the things that intrigue you, devote time and energy to, and have cultivated knowledge in. Please provide examples of your creativity and ideas along with your eagerness to share these with others so they may also learn from you.

Emma sent me a draft and said that her response was ninety-three words so she had room for seven more. This is what she came up with.

```
For the past five years, a nonprofit in my community,
started in memory of three young sisters has held a
5K race. Each year, I have organized a team that has
grown to over 100 people and raised countless dollars.
I created a different theme each year ranging from The
Shooting Stars to The Beautiful Butterflies. With a
minimal budget, I designed the costumes and selected
an inspirational quote. I am proud to say that we have
won the Spirit Award each year in recognition that our
enthusiasm captured the essence of the foundation.
```

In her email to me Emma worried about the essay. She wrote, "I feel as if I am not answering the question properly. I kind of feel as if they are asking for something specific. Do you think this adequately answers the prompt? Also, it seems kind of informational rather than showing my writing skills and personality?"

As I said earlier, we generally know what's not working in our writing. Emma was dead-on in her worries and it wasn't entirely her fault. The prompt is kind of crappy. The sentence structure is convoluted and confusing. I'm not sure what "expertise in imagination" means, for example.

Colleges want applicants to show what they're passionate about. Admissions people like to talk about passion, but it's become such a cliché that you see them straining not to use the *p*-word anymore. Most of us have things we're passionate about. When we love something, we try to learn as much as we can about it (fantasy football, origami using dollar bills, cheese), and then, because it excites us and we want to share our enthusiasm, we talk about it in ways that teach others and bring them into our weird, quirky obsessions.

So when I read this prompt I translated it to "What are you passionate about?"

Did Emma convey that in her short answer?

Well, no. And as she already knew, her essay was an information dump that showed nothing of her personality.

Let's be clear. This question is a beast to answer. Most of us don't think of our lives like this. We know what we like to do, but it can seem trivial, or boring, or typical. So I asked Emma to tell me in an email about anything she loves and wants to share with the world.

The thing that is most important to me and has been my whole life: the environment. It started out with my weird obsession with ducks. I just loved them! I collected hundreds of rubber ducks. On my preschool trip to a farm, I threw a temper tantrum because they wouldn't let me hold the baby ducklings. Then this photographer let me hold one and took a picture and I ended up on the front cover of the farm brochure in the spring! When I was little I also used to yell at my dad for not turning the water off while he brushed his teeth and made an effort to tell complete strangers to not litter. In addition, at my lake house, I stopped letting my grandma feed the ducks bread because I read that it hurt their stomachs.

Okay, this next bit tells me a little about Emma, but for an essay it's got too much of the precocious kid and not enough of the teen who is able to reflect on that little duck lover. At this point, one move Emma could have made would be to describe her child self using grownup language. Here's what I might have done.

I started out as a collector of rubber ducks and evolved into a poultry dietitian, not allowing my Nana to feed bread to ducks because it was bad for their GI tracts. Then I became a litter cop, yelling at strangers who dropped their Snickers wrappers on the ground. I monitored my dad's profligate use of water by turning off the tap while he brushed his teeth. In other words, from a young age I've been a kind of ecoterrorist.

That's just one move. There are plenty of others. She could layer in some reflection by writing, "I drove my family nuts when I insisted on stopping the car every time we passed a pond." That shifts the focus away from what she did (screaming) to how it affected others (drove them nuts). We have a smidgen of insight that lets us know that she's self-aware.

Another of Emma's short answer prompts was this:

Describe one or two examples of your academic or athletic experiences where you have considerably influenced your peers, helped resolve a conflict, or contributed towards a long-term group effort or goal.

She said she liked her first sentence: "Field hockey has become a significant part of what defines me."

Unfortunately, I found nothing to like about that sentence. What does it mean? Emma knew she needed a topic sentence and used one that put me right to sleep. Any girl recruited for field hockey could have written that opener. What if instead she'd written, "I'm the girl who sleeps with her field hockey stick and always has a ball in her purse." What if she wrote, "I'd rather play field hockey than go see Fitz and the Tantrums. And I love Fitz and the Tantrums."

Emma went on to describe how she'd spread the joy:

To share my love of the game, I based my Girl Scout Gold Award on it. I obtained free equipment from USA Field Hockey and with the help of my coach and teammates began clinics for the youth in my community. Coming from a small high school, the clinics allowed

```
me to introduce field hockey to the next generation of
players. I was able to teach my teammates to be leaders
and the younger girls to be team players while provid-
ing them with an opportunity to have a similar experi-
ence.
```

That's okay, though a bit on the generic side. I'm interested in *how* she taught her teammates to be leaders and the younger girls to be team players. What is the "youth in my community"? Was it teenage boys or six-year-old girls? Were the clinics every day or once a month? Had the young kids hit each other with their sticks? Did her teammates have to learn not to scream at them? Does she need to write "to share my love of the game"? Isn't that obvious? How does "coming from a small high school" fit in? As I asked her to add more details, I tried to show her the words and sentences that weren't earning their keep. It's always easier to write long and then cut.

Then I asked her to write me an email about why she loved field hockey. She said, "It saved me. I was headed down a dark and self-destructive road and field hockey was my saving grace. I would think to myself, 'If I do this, then I risk not being able to play field hockey.'"

I asked her to tell me about that dark road.

In a long email, Emma described her struggles over the past couple of years. The email was—I have to say this because it's true—a perfectly crafted essay, complete with a wonderful opening, vivid and specific details, insightful reflection, humor, topic sentences that introduced coherent paragraphs, and real and deep emotion without a shred of self-pity. There she was: the Emma I liked, respected, and admired, expressing the best, smartest version of her real and imperfect self.

Even though I'd told her repeatedly to write her essays as if she was emailing me, and even though she'd just read a draft of this book in which I say that same thing 8,453 times, I hadn't made myself clear.

She wrote back that she was confused: "I wasn't even trying to write an essay. That's all I have to do?" She added,

> I thought anything you write for college is supposed to be of the best quality. All I can think about is how the other kids will write better essays, have done better/ more things in their 17 years of life or just have a "leg up." That's what causes me to use words such as "obtained." I feel I need to seem extremely sophisticated and perfect. And that is because colleges are freaking intimidating! However, you've taught me I only need to be myself.

Emma is unique and special and wonderful and complex and kind and smart. She is also typical. Her anxiety about the process of applying to college got in the way of her ability to write good essays. I tried to show her that she knows what to do. If she reminds you of you, that's great. You couldn't be in better company.

Part Two

GETTING IT DOWN ON THE PAGE AND THEN CLEANING IT UP

7
Shitty First Drafts

THE IMPORTANCE OF ALLOWING YOURSELF TO WRITE BADLY

At this point, you may be thinking, *That's all very well and good in theory, Rachel. Easy for you to say, Ms. Bossyface. But I still don't know how to do this. I'm supposed to find a topic that will allow me to write like the best, smartest version of myself, and the essay is supposed to be about something other than what it's about, and I need to go to the shame, find and fill in the hole in my donut, and I need to be vivid and specific, and sure, maybe I can understand all of that, but I still don't know how to write the essay.* You might want to call me some nasty names right now, and you may be ready to throw this book across the room, because while you understand in theory what an essay is supposed to do, you have no earthly idea how to go about writing one.

Often in my creative writing classes I'll give students this assignment: Compose an essay about something—a job, a family member, a pet—and write as badly as you can (but still adhere to the rules of grammar).

They'll all laugh and say, "Oh, I can do that. I can write very badly."

Here's the funny part. These essays are usually fantastic. Once I've given my students permission to suck, they feel free to be creative and playful. When the stakes are low, they flourish. As soon as they think a piece of writing will be scrutinized and critiqued, however, they freeze up and produce an essay not nearly as good. That's why first drafts are so important. If I thought my writing had to be perfect—if I made sure each sentence was a polished jewel before I moved along—I'd never complete a draft of anything, even a text to my best friend.

Poop, Vomit, and Other Messes

A book I often recommend is Anne Lamott's *Bird by Bird: Some Instructions on Writing and Life*. It contains great instructions on writing (and life), and it's an entertaining read. Like all good writers, Lamott has a distinctive style—hers is sassy and funny.

The book gets its title from a story the author tells about when her ten-year-old brother had procrastinated on a homework project. He'd had three months to write a big report on birds. With the assignment due the next day, he sat at the kitchen table ready to cry.

Their father said: "Bird by bird, buddy. Just take it bird by bird."

That's terrific advice for any task that feels overwhelming. When I run a marathon I tell myself I only have to run one mile. Then I do another one. When you have to clean your room, you might turn it into a grid of one-foot-by-one-foot squares and clean a square at a time. Bit by bit, bird by bird.

One of my favorite chapters in Lamott's book is called "Shitty First Drafts." Here the author stresses the importance of letting your inner editor take a break. You just crank out what she calls "shitty first drafts." That's where you let it all out. No one will see it. You don't have to worry. She says a writer friend of hers calls it the "down draft," where you get it all down, and then, in the "up draft," you clean it up.

The message here—and it's a hard one for neurotic overachievers to choke down—is to give yourself permission to suck. You're writing your way into the essay, and you won't know what you think until you see what you say. That first version can wander and meander like a squirrel-crazed dog, darting off in unexpected directions. One of those directions might be something you really care about.

One of my undergraduate students once handed in an essay about free pianos. An abundance of free pianos is not a problem most of us have, but she worked in the office of a church and apparently fielded a number of calls from people offering their pianos for adoption. She started writing about free pianos, and then about what a pain it is to move a piano, and then she remembered a time when her brother offered to help move one of these freebies, and all of a sudden the essay was about her brother, about his ~~arrogance~~ confidence and how she couldn't believe other people didn't find him as annoying as she did.

She had written her way into the essay that mattered.

Probably 93 percent of the essays I read don't start where they start. Writers, even experienced ones, often begin with a bunch of warming up and throat clearing. Essays often start with the equivalent of a pianist sitting on the bench, pushing up her sleeves, and wiggling her fingers to get ready to play. That's part of the process, and it will help you get where you need to go. But eventually you'll need to learn how to come back and edit it out. I can't tell you how often I've made an arrow in the margin of the second or third paragraph, or on the second or third page, and asked, "Does the essay begin here?"

> Get it down. Take chances. It may be bad, but it's the only way you can do anything really good.
>
> WILLIAM FAULKNER

In your shitty first draft, you don't worry about where the essay starts or how it's structured or if it includes stuff that doesn't belong. You don't even think of it as an essay. You just write for yourself. You're writing to understand. You make associations, and at first the connections might seem random. That's fine. You're figuring stuff out as you go.

Write Your Way into an Essay That Matters

If I sit down to write about how much I love marshmallow Peeps, I might start with a celebration of the color yellow and how, really, all the other Peeps are wannabes. The only authentic Peeps are the yellow chicks, not the pink bunnies, nor Peeps for holidays other than Easter. Pumpkin Peeps? Please.

Writing only for myself, I might go on about other kinds of candy I love. Like Tootsie Rolls, and how I prefer the long thin ones to the little stubs or the giant logs that, when you open the wrapper, look like cat poop. I love caramel Bulls-Eyes with their weird flaky white middles. Candy corn. I might go on a rapturous riff about Halloween, which I think should be a national holiday.

Then I'll start thinking about why I love sweets so much. And why, in particular, I'd rather have a Junior Mint than a hand-dipped French truffle. Why do I prefer what most adults consider "kid candy"?

Oh crap, I'll say, as soon as I see where it's going. And then I'm writing about my father. When my brother and I were little, my father bet us that we couldn't go a year without eating candy. If we abstained, at the end of the year he would give us some amount of money—more than what the tooth fairy brought and less than the cost of a stuffed animal. The goal, he said, was to protect our teeth from cavities, and my brother and I complied. I ate no candy

> It is not the critic who counts; not the man who points out how the strong man stumbles, or where the doer of deeds could have done them better. The credit belongs to the man who is actually in the arena, whose face is marred by dust and sweat and blood; who strives valiantly; who errs, who comes short again and again, because there is no effort without error and shortcoming; but who does actually strive to do the deeds; who knows great enthusiasms, the great devotions; who spends himself in a worthy cause; who at the best knows in the end the triumph of high achievement, and who at the worst, if he fails, at least fails while daring greatly, so that his place shall never be with those cold and timid souls who neither know victory nor defeat.
>
> THEODORE ROOSEVELT

until I went to college, and then I went for the candy that little kids love.

In fact, the "bet" part was a ruse. My father had essentially commanded us not to eat candy. His parenting tactics, when I reached my self-hating teens, seemed harsh. Often he made me feel that nothing I did would ever be good enough to please him. So I became a hyper-overachiever. But my father never seemed satisfied with my efforts. The harder I tried, the higher he set the bar.

Now, as I write, I might wonder, *Why was he like that?* Why did he need to instill in me a drive for excellence? Was the candy bet about saving our teeth, or because *he* couldn't resist sugary treats and didn't want them in the house? Did he look back on his career and want a different—better—life for me? Had his father ridden him hard and that was the way he learned to show love? Was he unaware of how much he hurt me?

You can see how, by starting to write about something as trivial as marshmallow Peeps, if you allow associative leaps, let yourself make tenuous connections, and keep digging even when it feels uncomfortable, eventually you will hit essayistic gold.

Here's the key. In your first drafts, you need to become curious. About yourself and why you love what you love; about choices you made regardless of whether they were right or wrong; about the motivations of other people. And you need to be generous in your interpretations.

You can't mythologize yourself ("I was a straight-A student") or demonize others ("I had a crappy father"). And you can't be the victim ("I wasn't allowed to eat candy"). In her book *The Situation and the Story*, Vivian Gornick has a line that I love. In a good essay, she says, "we must see the loneliness of the monster and the cunning of the innocent." That means acknowledging your own manipulations and delving into the pain of those who may have hurt you.

In a shitty first draft, you're allowed to go crazy with unfettered emotion. You can fill fifteen pages with the love you feel for your puppy. You can point your finger at everyone who's ever cut in front of you in line or eaten the last piece of cake. You can blame your little brother for global warming and your mother for ruining your favorite song. No one will ever read this junk, so get it all out. Write with as much energy and passion as you can muster.

Then put that draft away. Shoot some hoops. Take your cat for a walk. Do homework. Then, in a week or so, have another look at it. You may become caught up in the emotions again, but this time get curious. Why should anyone care about how much you love your puppy? How will the reader feel if all you do is assign blame and take no responsibility for your own actions? Remember that when you point a finger at someone, you have three fingers pointing back at you. Can you find another way to look at the situation? Could there be a different, more generous interpretation?

While it's okay to be angry in a shitty first draft, the only way a rant can work on the page is if it's really, really funny. And as the actors like to tell us, dying is easy but comedy is hard. If you can talk about those impostors, the marshmallow bunnies and the hideous blue-colored chicks, while you defend the honor of yellow Peeps, go for it. But only if (1) you have a bigger point and (2) the reader will pee her pants laughing.

But that draft is an important step. If you keep writing, you'll likely get somewhere that may surprise you. You'll start to see connections. When I read over my first draft, the old cartoon light bulb might go on over my head, and I'll think: *Aha! No wonder when someone gives me candy, I feel loved.*

My father denied me the sweetness of treats, and he withheld affection. The stickiness of emotion made him twitchy. Far easier for him to command, even in the form of a thinly disguised "bet," than to discuss, negotiate, compromise. When, in my teens, I began to argue with him, he didn't know how to respond to my strong-headed stub-

> First, I do not sit down at my desk to put into verse something that is already clear in my mind. If it were clear in my mind, I should have no incentive or need to write about it. We do not write in order to be understood; we write in order to understand.
>
> CECIL DAY-LEWIS

bornness, my need to break free from his iron hand. Our relationship fell apart.

So as I continue to work on this shitty first draft, no longer angry, but with the dispassionate distance of an archaeologist sifting through the remains of a lost culture, I need to get curious. I might wonder what I had been missing. What if my father was doing the best he could, and because I couldn't see it at the time—and even for years afterward—I blamed him, unfairly, for, well, everything?

This, it turns out, is not the essay I expected to write when I sat to extol the virtues of (yellow) Peeps. What I'll have at the end is a bunch of pages of garbage, starting out with a too-long dissertation on candy and ending with a jumble of conflicted feelings about my father. It will be a big fat mess. I will never show it to anyone. I may feel stuck for a while.

After some time, when I've been able to digest these complicated thoughts, I'll be ready to start on another draft. And here's a weird dividend. By then my anger will have quieted and I'll be hit with a gee-whiz moment: maybe I need to forgive my father and myself. It turns out writing can be, well, therapeutic.

8
Seeing Again

REVISION MEANS RE-VISION

Many beginning writers claim they hate revising, or if they're honest, they might confess that they don't really know how to do it. Experienced authors will tell you that the most important step is revision.

When students look over their work, they tend to polish rather than revise. They'll fix the typos, put a comma in, take a comma out, do the hokey-pokey with some semicolons. They might substitute *colossal* for *big*. Polishing. Making things shiny and bright. Necessary, absolutely, but you need to take another more essential step first: revision.

Now I'm going to give you the best piece of advice I know about revision.

Warning: This may seem like the hardest thing in the world to do. It is. I promise that it works.

When you go to revise, reread your shitty first draft. Mark up the ideas that buzz in yellow highlighter, or stick a gold star on that part of the page, or draw $$$ signs in the margin, and then put that draft away (but don't throw it away). Think hard about what you've figured out, and write one sentence that captures the aboutness of the essay. And then:

Take a deep breath.

Open a new blank document.

Save it with a title.

And start writing.

I hear you screaming at me, and no, I'm not freaking kidding you. Yes, I'm sure you had some great stuff in that shitty first draft—exquisite sentences, vivid metaphors, ideas you might forget if you don't cut and paste them in.

Do not cut and paste.

I hear you wail, "I'll never write a sentence that good again."

You will. You will write one that's even better. Especially now that you know where you're going and what you want to say.

Yes, it sucks to start over. But this process is, I believe, the best strategy to revise short essays.

I learned this lesson the hard way. By dint of computer failure. I had written almost an entire book and then—NO!—the blue screen of death. Did I back up my work in those days before thumb drives, before the Cloud?

Do I floss every day?

I do not.

After I screamed and cried so loud my poor dog left the room, I got back to work.

And the work went surprisingly well. Since the book was nonfiction and based on a ton of research, I had my outline and my notes. I had to reconstruct everything I'd written before, and the new draft was much better than it had been.

At that point, I became a true believer in the new-blank-document school of revision. I had the confidence to know if I blew apart my first draft, I'd be able to put it back together, and the next draft would be a whole lot less shitty.

Let It Linger

Writing is so painful that even the most self-critical writer can feel a sense of relief after producing a draft, satisfied to have gotten to the end. It's difficult to look at that freshly laid egg and see it for the piece of chicken scratch it is.

That's why, after you've written a draft, you must put it away. Put it away long enough that when you come back to it you can ask yourself, *Who wrote this piece of dog doo?*

There are many reasons to start early on a writing project. Trust me, you will not do your best work three hours before it's due. When you spend a short amount of concentrated time on a piece of writing, going over and over it, you begin to memorize. Each sentence takes on a ring of inevitability, and the idea of changing anything becomes unthinkable.

But if you let a draft sit long enough, it can feel like it was written by someone else. When you come back to the page you'll find all sorts of sentences that don't make sense, and ideas that seem to come out of nowhere. Things that were clear when you wrote them will confuse you. Now you can make it better.

Murder Your Darlings

We tend to get attached to our creations. We toil to craft stunning, musical sentences. We come up with arresting, evocative images. We tell sidesplitting stories. And then, even if we realize they no longer belong in the essay, we have a hard time getting rid of them.

> Good writing is rewriting.
>
> TRUMAN CAPOTE

> Writing is hard work. A clear sentence is no accident. Very few sentences come out right the first time, or even the third time. Remember this in moments of despair. If you find that writing is hard, it's because it is hard.
>
> WILLIAM ZINSSER

None of the writing that goes into early drafts is ever wasted; it got you where you needed to go. But in revision you must be brutal. Novelist and critic Arthur Quiller-Couch wrote, "Whenever you feel an impulse to perpetrate a piece of exceptionally fine writing, obey it—wholeheartedly—and delete it before sending your manuscript to press. *Murder your darlings*." This advice is good, and difficult to heed.

Working on my second book, *The Pig and I*, I had a blast recounting the exploits of my pet pig, Emma. That little pork chop was a great character, and her adventures were hysterical. But my agent said, "These stories, while delightful, are all making the same point."

I'd gotten so attached to my own anecdotes that I forgot that every bit has to be doing some kind of work: deepening an argument, providing insight, or furthering the narrative. All my pig stories had the same message: "Look at funny Emma!"

I wanted to include five or six of them when one would suffice. It hurt me to delete those big blocks of text. I fought with my agent to retain more of them than I should have.

Now when someone tells me to murder my darlings, I do. I copy them into a separate document and label it "scraps." Someday I may be able to quilt those snippets into something beautiful. Or not. But I know the current piece will be better for what is left out.

9
Don't Try to Hook the Reader like a Trout

OPENING LINES

Once you know what your essay is going to be about and you're ready to revise, how should it start?

Many students believe they need a snappy first line to catch the attention of the reader. Often that goes wrong and results in the poor reader feeling like a trout played above a raging river—disoriented, confused, and traumatized. Instead of thinking about violently hooking or grabbing a reader, why not invite her into your world?

I like essays that begin with a simple declarative sentence. You might not think that's fancy enough. You might want to start in the middle of a scene with a zippy bit of dialogue: "'Let go of me!' I exclaimed loudly and excitedly."

Please avoid that impulse.

The Debutante with the Tattoo

Many years ago I worked with a girl named Lauren whose first draft started as follows:

```
The word "battante" stood out above the blinding white
of my petticoat, distinct like a hockey puck against
the ice. With a yelp, I noticed my visible tattoo and
yanked my hemline up to cover the little rebellion,
which in French means "fighter." In my corset-induced
```

delirium, I had imagined that the inked script had suddenly read "debutante"—and I nearly screamed.

Wait, what? Did that opening confuse you? It sure confused me. I couldn't figure out what was going on. Where was she? How did the word *battante* get onto the petticoat? Who wears a petticoat? What century are we in? Help!

As her next paragraph revealed, Lauren had gone shopping for fancy dresses with her "crazy Chinese mother and aunts." Then, at the start of the third paragraph, she wrote this line: "I am a Chinese / North Dakotan debutante with a tattoo, not something I had ever anticipated." That, I told her, could be her first line.

After nine drafts, Lauren's essay began:

I am a Chinese / North Dakotan debutante hockey player from Arizona with the word *battante* tattooed on my ass. I argue with theology teachers, refuse to give up in hockey games even when losing 12-1, and started the infamous boycott of the St. Thomas the Apostle Elementary cafeteria's "meatloaf." My road is typically the one less traveled. Everyone at my high school knows about my tattoo, which means "fighter" in French, but I would be flayed if my mother found out.

Using a word like *ass* might not work for a small evangelical Bible college. It might not have flown with her mom.

> My own experience is that once a story has been written, one has to cross out the beginning and the end. It is there that we authors do most of our lying.
>
> ANTON CHEKHOV

But in this case, given where she was applying (she ended up at Northwestern), I thought it was perfect. She could have written *butt*. Butt is funny. *Derriere* would have been awful.

I love that she used *infamous* to describe an elementary school boycott, and that she put meatloaf in quotation marks. Lauren understood what every writer knows: we like things in packages of three. In her second sentence, she gives a trio of examples: "I argue . . . refuse . . . started." *Flayed* is better than *skinned alive*. The rest of the essay went on to describe her battles with her mom, which was her aboutness.

Other Good Starts

I loved helping my college counselees find their first lines and opening paragraphs. Usually the good stuff came not from the stiff and stilted drafts of college application essays they'd worked hard on in class, but from emails we'd sent back and forth, or from phone conversations. I'd read through their messages, listen to them talk, and then say, "Hey! That's the first line of your essay." These tended to be simple, declarative sentences. Nothing fancy, just honest and straightforward sentiments.

Peter's early drafts, self-congratulatory and braggy, made me think he was kind of a jerk. I knew he wasn't a jerk. In his final essay he revealed himself as a chicken.

"Dậu" is my nickname. It means chicken. Not a commercialized agricultural chicken, but the kind of free-range chivalrous Asian chicken you find roaming on the streets of Siem Reap, Bangkok, and Saigon. Father's attempts at his dream—a successful barbershop—relocated us to Cambodia, Thailand, and halfway through my freshman year, America.

Jamie also began with what seemed like a triumphant chest-thump, but then he undercut it with a confession:

The only time I got the football in a high school game, I ran thirty-five yards and scored the winning touchdown. I left six Acton-Boxborough defenders sprawled on the ground. The crowd chanted, "Mouse! Mouse! Mouse!" and our quarterback locked me in a hug. The coaches never played me again. They said I was too small.

I'm partial to essays that answer the question "Who am I?" directly. I am this, and that, and that. A bunch of specific contradictions bundled together: I am a feminist who competed in a beauty competition. I am a vegetarian who eats bacon. I am a pacifist who wants to join the army.

But you might feel uncomfortable writing about yourself in this way. Instead, you may prefer to focus on other people. Here's the beginning of Rachel's essay:

My mother grew up in a poor rural town in Missouri. She was the first in her family to go to college and was determined to become a doctor. She worked her way through UMKC's six-year medical program, the only medical school she could afford, and spent years practicing as a dermatologist. She passed on her knowledge to me.

At the same time I was learning the alphabet, she was teaching me the ABCDs of melanoma: asymmetry, border irregularity, color variation, and diameter greater than 6 millimeters. My mother, strong, intelligent, and hardworking, embodied everything I wanted to be.

Rachel goes on to write about her mother's decision to leave dermatology and stay home with her kids. And then she discusses her sister. And then her brother. Rachel con-

> There is nothing to writing. All you do is sit down at a typewriter and bleed.
>
> ERNEST HEMINGWAY

cludes that each of her family members has traits she values, but that she's a different person and must find her own way, make her own mistakes.

As I said before, family is often a rich topic for an essay. Here's Max's opening:

> The most defining aspect of my world is my father. My mother often jokes that my father has the social skills of an engineer. He gets caught up in topics he's read about in health journals, and obsesses. They range from my sister and me spending too much time on the computer, which will "destroy our vision," to "too much mercury in salmon" to "getting headphones in order to avoid radiation from cell phones." These rants continue for about three months and then abate as another study comes out. He claims he is just concerned about his family's health, but my sister thinks he is out to embarrass his children by giving them health lectures in front of their friends. He certainly finds lots of ways to embarrass me.

Or you might want to write about someone who has meant a lot to you and whom you've never met, as Jane did:

> Many people experience middle school drama, a period of feeling completely alone. I was fortunate to experience it with someone by my side. She may not know me, but Taylor Swift helped me more than I could ever express.

What I love about that opening is that it starts dangerously close to "in society today, many children experience trauma in middle school." And it rubs up against the cliché of "my best friend helped me through a rough time." But Jane surprises us by telling us who helped her.

For the rest of the essay, Jane listed a song by Tay Tay and then described the event each song helped her deal with.

If you're having a hard time finding a badass first line, don't worry. Start writing and don't get too attached to your prose. Remember that an essay often doesn't start where it starts. You may not get going until the third paragraph, which was the case for Lauren's essay. As I've mentioned, on most of the essays I read, whether they're college application essays or graduate student work, I find myself drawing an arrow in the second or third paragraph, or on the second or third page, and asking, "Does the essay start here?" You need to learn to do this for yourself, or have someone read the essay and ask where he starts to get interested. Then cut everything that came before that point.

Find an opening that will set up the essay in a way that invites the reader in. Don't try to make it flashy or an attention-grabber. It should point us in a direction and introduce your voice. Most important, it should sound like you.

PEYTON'S ANKLE

What if you are fortunate to lead a relatively privileged life? Are you screwed when it comes to writing a good essay?

No. But you have to be self-aware. Remember those topics at the beginning of my students' lists? Those are the ones likely to produce the least interesting essays. They are usually as stale as five-day-old bread (cliché!). The equation of Activity = Life is hard to pull off because you have to write an essay that couldn't be written by any other ballet dancer, birder, or bowler. You have to reach hard for insight that doesn't come off as typical. That doesn't mean you can't make these topics work, but you'll need to realize how many others have written about feeling elated after catching the winning ball or being nervous when toeing the line before the start of the championship race.

You can do better than that.

Peyton, the daughter of one of my friends, told me she'd already written her essay, about going to Mexico on a mission trip and recognizing her own privilege.

Knowing that Peyton lives in a small town in Montana, I had an idea how much she had learned during that trip and was glad she'd had the opportunity to go. And because I know her dad, a man deeply committed to issues of social justice, I had the sense that she didn't need to leave the country to see how much more comfortable her life is than that of those who live in trailers five miles east of town, or thirty miles up the road on the Flathead Indian Reservation.

But I've read that community service essay 8,342 times. So has every admissions officer in the country. I knew that the trip, while important for her development as a person, was probably one of the least interesting things about her. For example, I knew Peyton was a dancer and had snagged the lead role in the *Nutcracker* three years running. I knew that she had spent the previous summer in New York City with the Alvin Ailey American Dance Theater, a largely African American company. And I knew her parents had split when she was very young and she had a complicated family life.

She also told me about her internship at a national parenting magazine. She said she wanted to go to law school. Then she told me about her ankle. Peyton has a condition that makes it painful for her to go *en point*. *Wow*, I thought. *And this cool girl wants to write a boring service-trip essay?*

Later her dad told me more about her ankle. One doctor said she could keep dancing on it. Another said she needed surgery. Her parents, who lived in different states, couldn't agree and went to court.

I gave Peyton a suggestion for the first line of her essay: "My parents went to court over my ankle." She could use the problems with her ankle to reflect on her evolution as a dancer, talk about the differences between ballet and modern dance, and ultimately, describe her challenging family situation. That's an essay I haven't read before.

You might think, *Hey, no fair! You gave her a great first line*. One of the things teachers do for students, and writers often do for each other, is make suggestions. I am rarely able to come up with titles for my own books or even my essays. They tend come from friends or from editors whom I ask for help when I get stuck. It's expected that you will ask for help, and it's okay to use a line someone else has given you after reading or listening to you talk about your essay. What's not okay is to have someone else write it. As I've said before, and I'll say again, the essay has to sound like you.

10
Danger!

SOME MOVES NOT TO MAKE

I've told you to steal, steal, steal the good stuff. You'll also need to identify moves that don't work. It's easy to see how our peers, our siblings, and people we feel competitive with go wrong in their writing. Swap essays with a friend. I guarantee that after you've read this book, you'll be able to find plenty of problems in his work.

To make that process easier, I'm going to give you a bunch of essay-writing proscriptions. These are the opposite of prescriptions. Instead of telling you what to do, here I'll warn you about what *not* to do.

That doesn't mean that you couldn't make any of these techniques work. An adept, confident writer can get away with all sorts of rule breaking. In essays published in magazines and on websites you'll see many of the moves I list here. Ask yourself, *Why did the writer make this choice? Is it serving her well? Or did she rely on a trick, a gimmick, a lazy cliché?*

Whenever I say in class, "Don't do this," chances are at least one rebellious student will do exactly that. Sometimes they succeed brilliantly and I'm thrilled. Often, however, they make the mistake I tried to save them from. I shake my head, smile, and attempt to avoid saying "Told you so."

Some of what I list here may seem obvious—stuff you would never do. And others may be moves you've made that you're particularly proud of, and you might feel a little stung when I tell you they're lame. Try not to take anything personally.

You Are There

I know professors of creative writing who will reject any applicant for graduate school who submits an essay about a past event written in the present tense. The most imperious of them will say, "This person clearly knows nothing about how nonfiction works."

I am not one of those people, though I know why they feel this way.

The present tense works in certain types of essays and books. Speeches and calls to action—Dr. King's "Letter from a Birmingham Jail," which you've probably already read three times by now—make it work. So do essays that perform what I call "thinking on the page," like William Hazlitt's wonderful 1826 essay "On the Pleasures of Hating." It begins, "There is a spider crawling along the matted floor of the room where I sit," and goes on to discuss how the haters gonna hate, hate, hate and why it's so much fun to do so.

Much magazine journalism is written in the present tense in order to give the reader a "you are there" sense. Here's how I might start a magazine profile: "Even sitting, Michelle Obama towers over me and makes me feel like a munchkin. I'm quaking like a dog at the vet just being near her."

Process essays explain how something works and are often in the present tense. If you want to read a great—and funny and profound—essay, look for Thomas Lynch's "The Undertaking." It starts, "Every year I bury a couple hundred of my townspeople." He's an undertaker—and a poet. How-tos, like this book, are written in the present tense. Lorrie

Moore's short story "How to Become a Writer," which you should google if you want to become a writer (or if you love reading good writing), starts, "First, try to be something, anything, else. A movie star / astronaut. A movie star / missionary. A movie star / kindergarten teacher. President of the World. Fail miserably. It is best if you fail at an early age—say, fourteen."

But when you're writing about events in the past, the present tense doesn't allow for reflection. What happened to you is less important than what you make of it. We want to see you reckon with what you've experienced and show how you've grown.

Because, well, the reader is always in it for herself. She's not all that interested in what happened to you. She wants to know what your experience can tell her about her. You need to take your particular and unique world and craft it into something universal. You want the reader to say, "This reminds me of me."

If the formula for a good essay is *tell a story; have some thoughts; lather, rinse, and repeat*, when you write in the present tense you leave yourself no room for those introspective moments. All you can do is tell the story. This happens, then this happens, then this happens. Some beginning writers think the present tense makes for more exciting reading. You'll see this is a fallacy if you pay attention to how many suspenseful novels are written in the past tense. You don't even notice as you read, turning page after page, staying up way too late.

Remember what I said earlier: in every personal piece about the past, even if the past was only two days ago, there are two characters named "I": the writer at the desk and the former self whose actions and thoughts you're recounting.

There's the you from the past, the you who is playing first base and daydreaming when the ball whizzes by your head and allows the opposing team to win the game. Instead of facing the disappointment of the team and your father, you run off the field to sulk like Achilles in his tent while the battle rages on. That you is not a happy camper.

As it turns out, though, you weren't just daydreaming. You were working on the lyrics to a song. A different version of you—the writer-at-the-desk you—figured out that baseball was never your passion. Your dad had been a minor league player. You never got to play with toy soldiers or trucks or dolls but only with gloves, bats, and balls. All your dad ever wanted was for you to play in college and beyond. And you never wanted to disappoint him. So you played. And you were good. Until that day, when the ball went streaking by and you realized you just weren't that into baseball. Music is what makes you want to get out of bed and what keeps you up at night. Music, not baseball. Maybe you didn't even know that was what you were thinking about when that line drive nearly took you out, but as you write the words "Now I understand," you do. You do understand.

The reader doesn't need to be in the present tense to feel the whoosh of air as the ball goes past. The immediacy that beginning writers think they purchase when they use the present tense often feels gimmicky and artificial. I'll say it again: the meat of the essay isn't what happened. The reader doesn't care about the ball—though we're likely to feel more fondly for the person who misses than the one who makes the heroic game-winning catch and brags about it. The reader wants to know why the play mattered. The Common App prompt asks, "How did [the failure] affect you, and what did you learn from the experience?" If you stick to the present tense, you don't get to figure out what you've learned.

Even though both characters named "I" are part of you,

one of them is in charge of bringing the insight. That's the job of the writer at the desk. But be generous to your past self. Treat the former version of you with compassion and understanding. Young you can't simply be an evil little witch who cared only about tormenting her little brother, or the guy who was too scared to dance. Your former self has to be as complex, as "round," a character as you can make him or her. You have to look at your former motivations and puzzle them out. The writer at the desk knows what's changed. The reader needs to be brought along, and not be subjected to some kind of dramatic switcheroo where the self-absorbed princess finally understands that she's a witch.

Tell your story. And then add the words "What I came to understand is" or "What I now realize" or whatever phrase you can come up with that gets you to think. When you revise, you may find too many instances of "What I now realize," and you'll edit them out. Use whatever it takes to get some insight on the page, and then be ruthless in your revisions.

The Essay Is Not a Mystery Novel

This brings me to the issue of suspense. In a first-person essay, you don't do yourself or your reader any favors by relying on a big reveal at the end. If you're writing about the past, we know you know how things turned out. You didn't die when you fell off the camel. Again, if you're focused only on the story part, you might be tempted to try to make it as exciting as possible and hold out on us. This may be a good impulse for a murder mystery, but for a personal essay, not so much.

It's fine to start an essay by telling us right at the beginning the biggest, most important (and possibly surprising) thing that happened:

```
My beloved horse died.

I missed the fly ball that lost us the championship
game.

In Burma I learned why imperialism is evil.

I'm an undertaker.
```

The element of suspense in an essay comes from us catching the writer in the act of revealing him or herself.

This is a hard concept for new writers to grasp, especially those who were raised on Stephen King or, in my case, Agatha Christie. We're used to plot being paramount. "Tell me a story," we beg our parents. We keep reading because we want to know what happens next. But in essays, the "plot" is less important than the changes we see in character. Again, look at those Common App prompts. They ask you to focus on change, on struggle, on failure, because that's where growth comes from.

Sometimes it can be useful, when you're writing about a memory, to do a shitty first draft in the present tense. I'm in favor of tricks that make the hard work of writing easier. And I'm also never going to tell you there's only one way to do something. If you want, close your eyes and think back to your favorite summer day at the beach. Remember the smell of the sunblock your mom made you slather on, and how the sand stuck to your feet and hurt when you walked on the pavement. Remember the whoosh whoosh whoosh of waves, and the salty taste of watermelon you'd picked up with hands that had just been in the ocean. Use all five senses to conjure everything you can remember.

Write it all. Know that most of it is junk you'll have to cut, but write to transport yourself back into the present of your past self. Then use that draft as you would use research material—figure out how to incorporate those vivid and specific details into the next version.

Does it make sense to start out in the present tense and then shift to the past? Well, you might be able to get away with it, but that's a move usually left best to experts. You do not want to confuse the reader; don't forget, the reader is easily confused. You never have a captive audience. I probably don't need to tell you that the easiest thing in the world is to put down a piece of writing that makes you work too hard. When you're forced to read books for school, you don't have the choice to opt out. But in real life, readers have lots of choices. A college admissions officer who needs to plow through hundreds of essays in a compressed amount of time will read quickly to see how much attention an essay deserves. If she starts out confused, she's going to be a whole lot less patient.

Leave Webster's Out of It

Unless you're using a word like *bubo* (armpit swelling) or *prink* (dress showily) or *demotic* (popular) or *couloir* (deep gorge), or *swipple* (loose part of a flail: *flail*, an instrument for threshing grain),[1] you can assume your reader probably knows the definition of words like *determination* and *procrastination*, and you're better off not starting your essay with "According to *Webster's Dictionary*, procrastination is . . ."

Even in the body of the essay, you don't want to define words we already know; you need instead to provide a deeper explanation. Chapters ago I mentioned an essay by one of my graduate students who wrote about two kinds

1. I got these from www.freerice.com, my favorite website, which helps you learn vocabulary and, for each answer you get right, donates ten grains of rice through the World Food Programme to a developing nation—you get smarter and you feed the hungry. Please take a few moments now and play some rounds of Free Rice.

> The road to hell is paved with adverbs.
>
> STEPHEN KING

of perfectionists: well adjusted and maladapted. She assumed we knew what perfectionists were, but she went further to make a distinction that became essential to the point of her essay and took it in an unexpected direction. She didn't quote any research but simply asserted the fact and then used it to make her point. That's a stealable move.

A good definition in an essay will reexamine a concept the reader thinks she understands and show how much more complicated things can be. We all know what the words *honor*, *generosity*, *racism*, and *courage* mean according to the dictionary. A good essay will extend that definition in ways that surprise the reader.

"Don't Do It!"

Many beginning writers love to start their essays with a snippet of dialogue. You see this all the time in published pieces, both good and bad. Again, you won't hear me say, "Don't ever do this," but I will caution that it's often a bad move and can leave the reader disoriented. Who is speaking? Why are we eavesdropping on a conversation?

It's true, one way to begin a piece of writing is by starting in medias res—in the middle of the action. *The Odyssey* begins not with Odysseus embarking on his journey but with a report of our hero held captive on Calypso's island. Like many great works of art, it relies on flashbacks to fill in the story.

Starting in medias res might be a good technique if you're writing an epic poem, but when you have only a limited number of words, it can be tricky to do well. Instead of dropping your readers into the middle of the action, bring them along by telling a story that starts at the beginning.

If you can't stop yourself from starting with a scene, do the reader a favor and set it up before you bring on the dialogue. People who want to write "creatively" often think that means including a lot of dialogue because they're used to reading novels, which tend to consist of more scenes than summary. Essays, on the other hand, can use both scenes and summary, and the summary can be more important. In the hands of novice writers, dialogue often goes awry because it's so hard to do well. My advice is to use it sparingly, or not at all.

Passive Voice

You know that every sentence needs a subject and a verb. What you may not have thought about is who is doing what to whom. Agency is the capacity to act.

Let's look at a sentence.

```
The bomb was dropped.
```

Nothing wrong with that (unless you're a pacifist).

The problem with the passive voice, though, is that it often lets the bad guys off the hook and doesn't give credit to those who deserve it. Fearful writers use it because they're afraid of assigning blame or because they don't know who is responsible. It's easier and safer to make it sound like an act of God, like "The rain fell." But that's boring to read. We need characters to feel engaged.

In the sentence above, the subject is *bomb*. The verb, *was dropped*. But where's the agent? Who dropped that bomb? The absence of the agent—the responsible person—marks the passive voice. Forms of the verb *to be* (in this case, *was*) are often markers of passive writing.

You could rewrite the sentence:

In 1945 President Harry S. Truman ordered an American airman on the *Enola Gay* to drop a five-ton hydrogen bomb on the Japanese city of Hiroshima.

Oh. That's a different story. We have a person (Truman) ordering an airman on board a plane to drop a load on a particular place. Isn't that more interesting?

Scientists love the passive voice. At least the older ones do. A sentence like "The experiment was performed" made sense because it shouldn't matter who performed it—the whole point of scientific research is doing procedures that are replicable. But now many of the best science journals are advising researchers to avoid the passive voice.

In a personal essay, the most important agent is you. So let me give you a more direct example.

Last summer will always be remembered by me.

Who else will remember what you did last summer?

My junior year began at a new school in Kent, Connecti cut.

Now this is not the passive voice, but it has a similar problem: it makes your junior year the agent. It shouldn't be. *You* began your junior year at a new school.

Avoid the passive voice. (Not "The passive voice should be avoided.")

Dangling, Modifying, and Too Much *Ing*-ing

You probably know what a dangling modifier is. They're often unintentionally funny sentences, like "Racing through the forest, the map got lost." What a dumb map. But at least it can race!

Whenever you start a sentence with an "ing" word, make sure that it refers to the right subject. In this case, you might add "we lost the map" after that comma. Were I to write that sentence, I'd be tempted to get rid of the *ing* altogether: "As we raced through the forest, the map fell and was lost." By inserting the actor (*we*) into that initial modifying phrase, you are free to give the main sentence any subject you please. In this case, *map* is the proper subject of the sentence.

When you use a participial phrase like "rushing to my computer," you need to be sure that whatever follows is concurrent—happening at exactly the same time. So if you next wrote, "I pounded out fifty pages of stellar prose," that would be a physical impossibility, unless you can type while you rush. Also, if you're writing about the past, I think it's cleaner to use the plain old past tense: "I rushed to my computer and pounded out fifty pages of stellar prose." People who have been taught to avoid using "I" to start sentences will often try to find ways around it. Don't worry. In a personal essay, your I is what it's all about.

There's nothing inherently wrong with *ing* words, but when there are a lot of them, it can feel as if the writer is trying too hard—rushing, rooting, peering, deciding—to make everything exciting and like it's all happening right now.

The Epigraph

Many works start with a quote from another writer. That's an *epigraph*. (Not an epitaph, which is what you'll find written on a tombstone.) In a short essay you probably don't need one. When you have a very limited amount of space, why give precious real estate to someone else's words?

Don't get me wrong. When I find a sentence or passage I love, I print it out and tape it above my desk. A snippet of good writing makes me want to write better. But I tend to leave those bits stuck on the wall, not in my own documents. In this book I have encouraged you to become a connoisseur and collector of beautiful sentences. I've quoted a bunch of my favorites throughout this book. You might want to start a new document, or use a blank notebook, and curate a gallery of sentences that make you swoon. Read them over when you feel stuck. This is the writer's equivalent of blasting get-psyched music before going out to a party.

Repeating the Prompt

Trust me, the admissions officers who read your essay are plenty familiar with the prompts on their applications. Instead of cutting and pasting the prompt, why not start by responding to it? Don't begin your essay, "*A time that I failed was* when I tried to beat up my little brother and I realized that he was bigger than me." You can start right in. "As I pulled my arm back to throw a punch, it struck me: he had gotten big. Bigger than me. So big that if I tried to clobber my little brother he could easily pick me up and throw me across the room." When you have a limited number of words, don't waste any telling the reader what she already knows.

Have You Ever Been Annoyed When a Writer Asks You a Question?

Rhetorical questions, or those that don't require an answer, can be powerful ingredients. However, like habanero peppers, they should be used sparingly.

```
What makes a good teacher?

Who decided that a woman's first job was to babysit?
```

Do you like being grilled? When you read, do you want the writer to tell you what she knows or ask you a bunch of irritating questions? Do you get impatient? In this book I've asked you, the reader, a lot of questions. That's because I'm giving you advice. I want you not just to read this text but to fully engage with it—to stop and think about how what I say here relates to your specific experience. As you go through this book, I want you to put it down often and come up with your own examples.

Instead of interrogating your reader, just relate your own experience. If you write, "Have you ever asked yourself what makes a good teacher?," you don't want the admissions officer to stop thinking about what you have to say and come up with his own answer. Don't ask questions; tell us what you think.

Introducing Yourself

As I've tried to drill into you, you must establish who you are on the page. But you don't do this the way you might when you meet someone in person. You don't want to start your essay by writing, "Hello, my name is ____." I can't believe how many emails I get from people whose name is right there on the "From" line and whose first sentence is "Hello my name is."

Of course, if your name is an important part of who you are, you might take a moment to meditate on that. "My name is Veruca because my mother loved Willy Wonka and thought it would be funny to name her kid after an unlikable child. This has shaped my life."

Sound Effects

Thwack! Whizz! Whoooosh! Pow!

Are you thinking of comic books? I am. Certainly good writing can benefit from a little onomatopoeia—the use of a word that suggests the sound it describes. *Clunk* is a good one. Or *meow*. Or *fizz*. But once you start overdoing it and adding exclamation points, especially in the first words of your essay, you're wading into troubled waters. You're in danger of making the reader cover her ears with her hands. I beg you, do not start your essay with a *Bang!*

Floating Body Parts and Busy Inanimate Objects

One way to make your reader giggle is to give body parts their own agency.

When you write a line like "His hands threw up," I get a visual image of hands barfing. That is not a pretty picture; it's strange and yucky. Body parts don't have actions of their own. I probably don't need to do more here than give you some examples:

My eyes fell to the floor. *Ouch. I bet that hurt.*

His eyebrows jumped in surprise. *Athletic eyebrows!*

In a similar manner, objects can't move on their own. "Heavy boots clomped down the hall" might make for a good scene in an animated movie, maybe one with magical boots. But in an essay, the boots have to be worn by a person.

A cabin rests on the top of a hill. *Did it get tired from walking?*

Descriptions of Yourself from Outside of Yourself and Self-Quoting

"I grimaced at my computer screen." Who is watching you as you type? Why did you grimace? Here a writer is trying to show—what? Frustration? Pain? You might say of someone else that they grimaced and let us try to infer what they're feeling. But in the first person, we expect you to tell us what you feel. And think.

One of the ways first-person essays can clang is when a writer quotes herself too much or shows herself from a third-person perspective. We know you were there. We know you were talking. Own your "I."

The Confessional Ick

In this book I've urged you to be honest. I've tried to convince you that the best writing comes when you strip yourself down, take off the armor, and show who you are.

That does not mean, however, that you need to share with us your most, um, intimate thoughts or actions. In fact, I've read too many essays that make me go *Ick*. I don't want to hear about the colors you puked up when you drank too much Southern Comfort, or about how you love to pop your zits, or a step-by-step description of your sloppy first kiss. You have to maintain a fine balance between letting the reader in and dancing around in your underwear.

Clichés Think Your Thoughts for You

You already know you're not supposed to use clichés, those tired old phrases that you've heard and read so many times. My buddy George Orwell said that the problem with clichés is that they "think your thoughts for you." They make our language stale and lifeless. When phrases become clichés, they cease to evoke a visual image. Is it tow the line or toe the line? What visual image does that phrase conjure for you? Do you see a sailor holding a rope attached to a ship and somehow dragging it? Or do you see a runner at the start of a race, putting one foot out and getting ready to go? (It's *toe*.)

Most of our English clichés come from two sources: good old Willie the Shake and the King James Version of the Bible. I first read the Bible in a college English class. Was I ever surprised to see that it was filled with beautiful language—and tons of clichés. Like these:

bite the dust
the blind leading the blind
by the skin of your teeth
drop in a bucket
nothing but skin and bones
see eye to eye
there's nothing new under the sun

Think hard about that last one. There is nothing new under the sun. We steal phrases and thoughts all the time. From Shakespeare, the Bible, movies, and TV. You may not realize, however, when you are. There's an old joke about the guy who saw *Hamlet* for the first time. He said he liked the play, but too bad it was filled with clichés. Orwell's advice is "Never use a metaphor, simile, or other figure of speech which you are used to seeing in print." If you're un-

A writer is a person for whom writing is more difficult than it is for other people.

THOMAS MANN

sure, give your essays to a bunch of readers and ask them to scout for clichés.

Clichés of Thought

Some clichés go beyond language; they are stale thoughts on worn-out topics. Admissions officers have read certain kinds of essays so many times they come to dread them. I've warned you against these throughout the book.

```
I've wanted to be a doctor since I was four years old.
```

```
My mom is the best mom in the world.
```

```
I'm a dedicated worker.
```

You're not a kid anymore. So put away childish things (that's also a quote from the Bible), and start from the person you are now. An essay I'd want to keep reading might start, "I wanted to be a doctor since I was four years old. But last year, when I took biology, I realized I still wanted to be a doctor but for completely different reasons."

Spellcheck Is Your Friend, and Can Also Make Nonsense of Your Prose

At this point it should go without saying that you need to pay attention to the red and green squiggly lines Microsoft puts under some of your words. There's no excuse for misspellings. Apple's Pages program even points out clichés. Those are useful tools, and tools are your friends.

However, this doesn't mean that when all the words are spelled correctly, they are the words you want or mean. When I need a giggle, I google "autocorrect fails." Our devices are getting smarter and funnier all the time. No word-processing program would catch a line like "I want to go to Duke instead of a big pubic university."

When I read that sentence in an application, I cackled so loudly my colleagues came running down the hall to see what was wrong. Then we all laughed together. At the student, not with him.

Homophones are words that sound the same but have different meanings. You know, like *flour* and *flower*; *kneads* and *needs*; *dyes* and *dies*; *peaked*, *peeked*, and *piqued*. We have zillions of them in English, and they will get you into trouble if you're not careful.

More Advice from George Orwell

In case you've ignored my repeated counsel to google "Politics and the English Language," I'm going to give the last word in this chapter to Uncle George. Here's a digest of his advice in that essay:

```
A scrupulous writer, in every sentence that he writes,
will ask himself at least four questions, thus:

   What am I trying to say?
   What words will express it?
   What image or idiom will make it clearer?
   Is this image fresh enough to have an effect?

And he will probably ask himself two more:

   Could I put it more shortly?
   Have I said anything that is avoidably ugly?
```

At the end of the essay he adds,

I think the following rules will cover most cases:

Never use a metaphor, simile, or other figure of speech which you are used to seeing in print.
Never use a long word where a short one will do.
If it is possible to cut a word out, always cut it out.
Never use the passive where you can use the active.
Never use a foreign phrase, a scientific word, or a jargon word if you can think of an everyday English equivalent.
Break any of these rules sooner than say anything outright barbarous.

11
Semicolons Are like Loaded Guns

MECHANICS MATTER

If I were Queen of the World, or Oprah, I would give a present to every high school student: a copy of *The Elements of Style*. When I assign this book in my college classes, students have two reactions. First they're embarrassed to see how many mistakes they make. Then they get kind of indignant and ask, "Why hasn't anyone told me to read this before?"

"Probably someone did," I say. "But you didn't know it would be so much fun."

Please order a copy right now. Or check one out of the library. Read it, cover to cover, in one sitting. Then reread it every year. I do. And every time I'm reminded of mistakes I continue to make. Most people refer to this little book not by its title but by the names of the authors: Strunk and White. You know E. B. White. You've read his book *Charlotte's Web*, and maybe *Stuart Little*, and I've mentioned his essay "Once More to the Lake." Believe me when I tell you, *The Elements of Style* is a fun book.

Here's a sample:

> *Rather, very, little, pretty*—these are the leeches that infest the pond of prose, sucking the blood of words. The constant use of the adjective *little* (ex-

```
cept to indicate size) is particularly debilitating;
we should all try to do a little better, we should all
be very watchful of this rule, for it is a rather im-
portant one, and we are pretty sure to violate it now
and then.
```

For all the many people who love this book, some English professors and others hate it and find it bossy. I like Strunk and White because it's short (less than 100 pages) and funny and contains useful reminders.

You know who else loves it? Stephen King—yes, *that* Stephen King. If you don't want to read Strunk and White, get King's excellent and engaging book *On Writing*, which gives much the same advice and also tells you how he became *that* Stephen King.

Silly mechanical errors will undermine your authority as a writer. I want you to care about your sentences on many levels. I want you to recognize a beautiful sentence when you see (or write) one, and I also want you to write in ways that are grammatically correct. I know your readers—including whoever reads your admissions essay—will judge you if you seem careless.

The great Joan Didion said, "Grammar is a piano I play by ear." Same for me. I'm not going to give you the fancy names or explanations for linguistic constructions. I'll just say that in addition to Strunk and White and *On Writing*, there are tons of style guides and websites that will teach you the basic rules. Find one you like and study it. In the meantime, here are tips for avoiding some common mistakes.

Read Aloud

The best way to revise your prose is to read your work out loud. Not just moving your lips as you go over it, not mumbling as if you're talking to a friend in church. I mean, out LOUD. What you'll find is that you will stumble over some of your sentences. You'll need to fix them. When we read aloud we can serve as our own autocorrect.

Better yet, make a copy and have someone else read it aloud while you follow along. Note the places where they stumble or inadvertently correct errors. Put a big *X* by the spots that make you cringe, and then go back and revise like crazy.

Paragraph Breaks Are Your Friends, and Your Readers' Friends

How can you be kind to your poor readers? You can make reading for them as easy and as pleasurable as possible. That means, in addition to all the things you've been learning in this book (be specific; use vivid language; tell a story, then have some thoughts; fill the hole in your donut), you must break your prose into paragraphs.

Yes, paragraphs. Each should start with a topic sentence that points the reader to the most important point you want to make, like "Mocha Miss was an asshole." In that paragraph you will give us specific and vivid examples of how the horse got on your last nerve.

Then you'll give the reader a break. Start a new paragraph. That one might begin, "She was an asshole, but I

> If you have any young friends who aspire to become writers, the second greatest favor you can do them is to present them with copies of *The Elements of Style*. The first greatest, of course, is to shoot them now, while they're happy.
>
> DOROTHY PARKER

loved her. I loved the way she tried to eat my hair. I loved that she rested her chin on my shoulder when I picked out her feet. I loved that when she heard my voice in the barn, she'd start nickering." You'll set us up in the first sentence to know what's coming next.

Just as readers need paragraph breaks to give them some breathing room, they also need to be able to breathe when they're reading. That's where commas come in. You want to keep tight control over your sentences and vary their structure. Short sentences are great. But sometimes, especially when you're trying to slow the pace, you want to let the reader linger on the points you are making, to invite her to come with you on a journey of discovery, and in those cases your sentences might amble along, relaxed and loose. (Reread that last sentence without the commas and you're likely to feel like you just sprinted 100 meters.) If you read the piece aloud and exaggerate the pause on each comma, you'll have a good idea if the commas are in the right places.

The Quotation Mark Dance: Periods and Commas Go INSIDE

To those students who think it's stupid to spend time learning correct spelling, proper punctuation, and the rules of grammar, here's my response: it's not that there's any absolute logic to the way we do things, but if you don't adhere to accepted standards, you will look stupid. It's that simple. Yes, we could debate whether it's more reasonable to put periods and commas outside of quotation marks, but the fact is, American convention dictates that they belong inside. Until the convention changes, that's where you should put them.

This is correct: "Put them inside," I say.

This example is incorrect (but it happens in real life

when I teach class): “If students get punctuation wrong I make them do a dance”.

Periods and commas go INSIDE quotation marks, people. Even when it looks funny. Like this,

```
She said, "I just read 'The Dead.'"
```

Colons and semicolons go OUTSIDE quotation marks.

Question marks move around, depending on where the question is. Sometimes it’s part of the quote, so it goes inside, like this:

```
"Do you want to go?" she asked.
```

But it can also linger outside:

```
Did she just say, "I want to go"?
```

Exclamation Points! Where Do They Go?!

You may think exclamation points follow the same rule—that they go where they belong relative to the quote. That’s true, but here’s what I think: Exclamation points shouldn’t be used. Except maybe in texts and emails. Exclamation points are the refuge of the weak and the lazy writer. They’re needy. They scream, “Like me!” You should use syntax and word choice to make exclamations. Though yes, I know, I have used them in this book, mostly when I’m trying to seem less bossy—more friendly aunt than fascistic English teacher.

Run-On Sentences and the Abuse of Semicolons

Run-on sentences are a danger when you try to get fancy or when you’re not thinking about the reader. Comma splices happen when you ask that punctuation mark to do the heavy lifting of a period or a semicolon or a conjunction. That is, when you have two independent clauses that could easily stand on their own, either you can end the first one with a period or, if the thought is closely connected, you can add a semicolon, kind of like a bridge that joins two sovereign islands. Or you can connect them with an *and* or a *but*.

Here's a comma splice:

```
Learning English punctuation isn't hard, you just have
to pay attention.
```

Can you see that poor comma straining under the weight of trying to keep those parts together? Its biceps are starting to shake. It's teetering, about to cave in. All you have to do is swoop in and shore it up with a stronger punctuation mark.

```
Learning English punctuation isn't hard. You just have
to pay attention.
```

Ah. Can you hear the sigh of relief?

Or

```
Learning English punctuation isn't hard; you just have
to pay attention.
```

Or

```
Learning English punctuation isn't hard, but you have
to pay attention.
```

Note this: semicolons are like loaded guns. They are powerful marks that should be used only by those who've received training. They are not commas on steroids. They seem intimidating and sophisticated. Unless you can use them as naturally as you can breathe, please don't. Shorten your sentences. Connect independent clauses with conjunctions. Leave semicolons to the experts.

Capitalization Fetish

Sometimes when I take a quick glance at a student essay I think it's in German. In that language, all nouns, not just proper names, are capitalized. Random and incorrect capitalization can make your prose look silly. In English, *high school* is not capitalized, unless it's part of a proper noun (an official name): Mayberry High School. Classes like biology and chemistry should be in lower case. English is the name of the language we're studying, and it deserves a big *E*.

What do you do if you're uncertain about whether or not to capitalize? First, congratulate yourself for caring enough to think about it. Then, look it up. Learn the rules. You too can become a linguistic terrorist and drive yourself crazy when you go to restaurants and can't help but edit the menus. For some reason, restaurant people love to capitalize.

I've also noticed a weird fetish for using quotation marks.

```
Eat here for "good food."
```

Is that because they don't think their food is actually good?

Unless you're using someone else's words, you generally don't need quotation marks.

Between You and Me

When I watch the reality TV shows I love so much, I notice people trying to appear sophisticated by using *I* instead of *me*. Incorrectly.

An editor at the *New Yorker* magazine wrote a terrific book called *Between You and Me*. The author, Mary Norris, is annoyed when people commit the sin against language of using *I* when they should use *me*. I share her irritation.

If you say "just between you and I," you're going to sound ignorant. It should be "between you and me." If you say "He showed it to Joe and I," I'm going to say, "No, he didn't." It's "He showed it to Joe and me." All of the contestants on *The Bachelor* need to read Norris's book.

Here's a quick way to figure out what's correct. Take out the other person. In the sentence above, take out Joe. Would you write "He showed it to I"? Didn't think so.

Between You and Me is a fun book that explains how not to make many such common mistakes. If you think it's boring to read about punctuation, google Lewis Thomas's short essay "Notes on Punctuation." Here's the first paragraph:

> There are no precise rules about punctuation (Fowler lays out some general advice (as best he can under the complex circumstances of English prose (he points out, for example, that we possess only four stops (the comma, the semicolon, the colon and the period (the question mark and exclamation point are not, strictly

> The most valuable of all talents is that of never using two words when one will do.
>
> THOMAS JEFFERSON

```
speaking, stops; they are indicators of tone (oddly
enough, the Greeks employed the semicolon for their
question mark (it produces a strange sensation to read
a Greek sentence which is a straightforward question:
Why weepest thou; (instead of Why weepest thou? (and,
of course, there are parentheses (which are surely
a kind of punctuation making this whole matter much
more complicated by having to count up the left-handed
parentheses in order to be sure of closing with the
right number (but if the parentheses were left out,
with nothing to work with but the stops we would have
considerably more flexibility in the deploying of
layers of meaning than if we tried to separate all the
clauses by physical barriers (and in the latter case,
while we might have more precision and exactitude for
our meaning, we would lose the essential flavor of lan-
guage, which is its wonderful ambiguity ))))))))))))).
```

Funny, right? So many errors creep into our prose. Ask your teachers or parents or friends to point out your bad habits. Do you have a comma abuse problem? Do you fetishize semicolons? Are all your sentences too long or too short? Pay attention: your readers will.

12

My Little Bag of Writing Tricks

SOME TIPS

Many writers are technically competent, don't make any of the dumb moves I've warned you about, and know the rules of grammar and punctuation. That makes their writing correct—but not necessarily good. You may understand what they've written but not enjoy reading it.

First, go for clarity. You want your mechanics to be perfect. But then you want your sentences to sing. When you have space for only a limited number of words, as you do in an application essay, you need to make each of them count.

I hate excess. I can't stand clutter. I always write long and then take pleasure in hacking away as much as I can, using a routine of tricks to make sure my prose isn't too flabby.

First I hit Control F and look for forms of the verb *to be*. In case you've forgotten, here they are:

am
are
is
was
were
be
being
been

There's nothing wrong with these words. You can write perfectly good sentences using them.

```
The essay was written by a student. It was amazing and
delightful.
```

Those sentences are fine. Could they be better? Of course. At a certain point, you want to go beyond correct. You want to create energy in your prose.

If you get rid of the *to be* verbs, you can enliven your work.

```
The student's essay amazed and delighted me.
```

We've moved from a static description to a sprightlier construction, and we cut the word count almost in half. We also added in a human. Me. If you hear something is amazing and delightful, you might want to know who believes that.

Go on a mission with one of your essays. Search for all the forms of *to be* and see what you've got. Now try replacing each of them with a more vigorous verb. Better? Shorter? Sprightlier?

Qualifiers

Whenever I finish a draft, I know I'll have to Strunk-and-White myself and do some qualifier weeding. I hit Control F and search for *very*, *little*, *pretty*, *really*. Sometimes my entire screen lights up in yellow highlighted words and I think, *Oops. Got a little lazy there, Rachel? You REALLY need to be more careful. This is VERY bad writing*. Then I go on a search-and-destroy mission for *justs*.

Let me be clear. You can use these words. But as with everything, be deliberate. What work are these *littles*, *verys*, and *prettys* doing? Could I make the sentences stronger by deleting or replacing them? Often we put them in to soften our opinions. I might write "You got a little lazy" because it sounds friendlier than "You got lazy." If you wipe out freeloader words that aren't earning their keep, you will have more space for complicated ideas and vivid descriptions.

Adverbs Are Not Your Friends

I also go on to ferret out those weaklings, adverbs. I do this by Control F-ing "ly." If I find a place where I've written "He laughed loudly," I might change it to "He roared." Or "He squealed." Good writers tend to rely on strong nouns and verbs. There are important uses for adverbs and for what are called, in grammatical terms that are beyond my comprehension, adverbial phrases. You can get someone else to explain that to you. For our purposes, I'll just say that I try to choose each of my words with care. I know that when I get lazy I tend to hastily, thoughtlessly, and sometimes randomly add adverbs that don't do me any favors.

Word Packages

So many times I have read in a student paper, "For all intensive purposes." That is a meaningless phrase written by someone who has misheard "for all intents and purposes."

Because it comes in a package, we don't bother to unpack it. We use it without thinking. Like "tried and true." What about "free gift"? What other kinds of gifts are there?

Look at this list of redundancies. Now look at your own writing and see if you're saying the same thing twice, or qualifying a word that doesn't need it.

personal beliefs
true facts
final outcome

first and foremost
consensus of opinion
very unique
each and every
regardless of whether or not

Junk Phrases

Now look at this list.

owing to the fact that
is the reason for
on the grounds that
this is why

All of these could be shortened to *why* or *because*. And now these:

is able to
is in a position to
has the opportunity to

All reduce to *can*. You don't need the extra words.

Decluttering

When I'm going over my final draft, I do a search for three words: *this*, *that*, and *there*. Then I ask myself if eliminating them will make my prose leaner.

This is why my birthday matters to me → My birthday matters to me
It is important *that* you understand → You must understand
There is a need for more study → We should study

See how the *this*, *that*, and *there* aren't necessary?

You can also see how the *there is* comes before a vague noun, and if you search for *there*s you'll often find them followed by a *to be* verb. In a shitty first draft, I'll get the ideas on the page and include a lot of *this*es, *that*s, *there*s, *to be* verbs, *very*s, *little*s, *just*s, and a whole bunch of other junk. Then I go through and clean up using Control F. I'll try to notice if there are words I use frequently and do a search for them. I'll check for too much *ing*-ing. I can get rid of many needless words this way.

Then I operate on another level. When I write something like "She nodded her head," I'll think, *What else would she be nodding?* So off with *her head*. "She nodded." Or "He shrugged his shoulders and sat down." What else would he shrug? How else would he sit? I could revise that to "He shrugged and sat." I'm not saying you always want to get rid of extra words; just make a conscious decision about each one.

Pretension by Latin

A painful part of my revision process is to hunt down places where I'm working too hard to sound smart. If I have passages where I use a bunch of fancy language, I know I'm probably covering up some fuzzy thinking. This goes back to George Orwell's preference in "Politics and the English Language" for good old Anglo-Saxon words over Latin and Greek. You may not think you know the difference, but you do. Short words that are closer to the body and its functions, that tend to be vivid (and sometimes dirty), are from the Anglo-Saxon, unlike the more abstract terms, often with lots of syllables that end in *-ize* or *-ate*, that come from Latin.

Once I was hiking through Canyonlands National Park in Utah with a geologist future ex-boyfriend.

Elmore Leonard:

» Never use a verb other than "said" to carry dialogue.

» Never use an adverb to modify the verb "said" . . . he admonished gravely.

» Keep your exclamation points under control. You are allowed no more than two or three per 100,000 words of prose.

» Never use the words "suddenly" or "all hell broke loose."

» Use regional dialect, patois, sparingly.

» Avoid detailed descriptions of characters.

» Don't go into great detail describing places and things.

» Try to leave out the part that readers tend to skip.

Neil Gaiman:

» Write.

» Put one word after another. Find the right word, put it down.

» Finish what you're writing. Whatever you have to do to finish it, finish it.

» Put it aside. Read it pretending you've never read it before. Show it to friends whose opinion you respect and who like the kind of thing that this is.

» Remember: when people tell you something's wrong or doesn't work for them, they are almost always right. When they tell you exactly what they think is wrong and how to fix it, they are almost always wrong.

» Fix it. Remember that, sooner or later, before it ever reaches perfection, you will have to let it go and move on and start to write the next thing. Perfection is like chasing the horizon. Keep moving.

» Laugh at your own jokes.

» The main rule of writing is that if you do it with enough assurance and confidence, you're allowed to do whatever you like. (That may be a rule for life as well as for writing. But it's definitely true for writing.) So write your story as it needs to be written. Write it honestly, and tell it as best you can. I'm not sure that there are any other rules. Not ones that matter.

P. D. James:

» Increase your word power. Words are the raw material of our craft. The greater your vocabulary the more effective your writing. We who write in English are fortunate to have the richest and most versatile language in the world. Respect it.

» Read widely and with discrimination. Bad writing is contagious.

» Don't just plan to write—write. It is only by writing, not dreaming about it, that we develop our own style.

» Write what you need to write, not what is currently popular or what you think will sell.

» Open your mind to new experiences, particularly to the study of other people. Nothing that happens to a writer—however happy, however tragic is ever wasted.

As we scampered along talking about this and that, a lizard improbably scooted right under my hiking boot as I took a step.

I murdered a lizard. This made me feel horrible.

My future ex-boyfriend said, "We could fabricate a tiny cross by the side of the trail to mark the spot."

I said, "Why would you say something like that?"

He said, "I thought it was funny. You know, like the markers they erect on the sites of highway fatalities."

I said, "No. Why would you say *fabricate*?"

He looked confused. "Because that's what I meant."

I gestured toward the natural beauty that surrounded us. "Why wouldn't you say *make*, or *build*?"

"Because," he said, getting insistent and treating me like an imbecile, "that's not what I meant. I used a more precise word."

"They mean exactly the same thing," I said. At this point I may have been screaming.

Fabricate is no more technical than *make*. My future ex-boyfriend didn't understand the difference. Nor did he understand how he used the language of science to distance himself from bodily human experience, even while hiking in a magnificent national park. Doctors ask us to *urinate* in a cup, not *pee*. Scientists *inquire* rather than *ask*. Philosophers don't *think*, they *cogitate*. None of the fancy words are more precise than the simple ones that have the same meaning.

```
endeavor → try
utilize → use
initiate → start
cognizant of → know
facilitate → ease
deem → believe
```

Both Latinate and Anglo-Saxon words have a place in our prose, though like Orwell, I am partial to language that is clear and direct and doesn't try for fancy. I like the sound of *gut* better than *abdomen*. I like to *chew* instead of *masticate*, to *drink* rather than *imbibe*, and I prefer to *want* rather than *desire*. My dog Helen *farts*, she doesn't become *flatulent*. I'd rather *lie* than *prevaricate*, though as you know by now, I believe honesty is the best policy.

Zombie Nouns

Another linguistic tic I try to keep out of my prose is to rely on nominalizations. You may prefer the term *zombie nouns*. I know I do.

What is a nominalization or zombie noun? Abstractions that suck the life out of writing. How do they do this? By turning a perfectly good verb into a noun. Like this:

```
The police conducted an investigation.
```

What, exactly, does an investigation look like? Good question. Do you get a visual image?

What if we said instead, "The police investigated"?

Or

```
The police searched.
```

Or

```
The police grilled bystanders.
```

Or

```
The police comforted the victim.
```

A more vigorous verb gives a better picture of what's going on and who is doing what.

Instead of writing "A decision was reached to break up," you might think harder. Who reached the decision? How? When you write a sentence like that, go back and ask yourself what you're trying to hide. It might be

```
After hours of laughing, crying, and talking until we
were hoarse, I decided to break up with John.
```

I go through my document and look for words that end in *-ment*, *-tion*, *-ity*, *-ism*, typical suffixes for nominalizations. I look at each word that describes something abstract and ask myself if that's the one I want to use. In some cases, it is. And in others, I change it.

If you still don't understand the problems with pretentious word choice, here's another example from Orwell's

"Politics and the English Language." He takes a beautiful chunk from the biblical book of Ecclesiastes:

> I returned and saw under the sun, that the race is not to the swift, nor the battle to the strong, neither yet bread to the wise, nor yet riches to men of understanding, nor yet favour to men of skill; but time and chance happeneth to them all.

And then he translates it into something my future ex-boyfriend might have written:

> Objective considerations of contemporary phenomena compel the conclusion that success or failure in competitive activities exhibits no tendency to be commensurate with innate capacity, but that a considerable element of the unpredictable must invariably be taken into account.

No one wants to write like the undead.

The Shape of the Thing

When I was a young editorial assistant at a publishing house, my job was to read manuscripts and write reports on them. After they were logged in, the secretary placed them on a long, low cabinet. Each day I stood and surveyed my choices. In order to decide what I wanted to tackle next, I'd pick up a manuscript and leaf through it. Without reading a word, I could tell which ones would be painful and which I could get through quickly.

I put off reading manuscripts packed with text as dense as a nineteenth-century novel, with monstrous paragraphs that went on for days, with little white space and no subheads. Those manuscripts gave me a headache before I even brought them back to my office.

Instead I'd look first for easier reads, whose authors kept my experience in mind by creating pages that looked inviting, that promised to hold my interest and also give me a break.

Here's a piece of advice I've stolen from another author: *Don't write like a suburb.* You want your work to be intriguing from the outset. A bunch of paragraphs of identical size and shape, plotted out like a planned community, will be less enticing than an essay whose structure looks like a map of Lower Manhattan or Paris.

When I'm finishing a draft, I shrink View to 50 percent and scroll through to see how it looks. If it feels too blocky, I try to break it up.

Do whatever you can to make your text look like an appealing read.

And While We're at It, Here Are Some Rules to Ignore

In your English classes, you may have to follow a long list of rules that your teacher says are necessary for good grammar. I beg you to ignore these. You'll have already noticed that I do.

Never begin a sentence with *But* or *And*. (Remember Dr. King's long sentence? It starts with *But*.)

Never use contractions.

Never refer to the reader as *you*.

Never use the first-person pronoun *I*.

Never end a sentence with a preposition.

Never split an infinitive.

Never write a paragraph consisting of a single sentence.

CONCLUSION

Getting It Done

Because I'm committed to telling you the truth, I'm going to give you some bad news about writing.

It never gets easier.

You can often find me whining about how hard it is to write. I collect quotes about this, which you've seen throughout this book. It helps me to know that many great writers—whose gorgeous prose reads as effortless—struggle as much as I do. While it never gets easier, most of us learn some tricks along the way, develop habits that ensure that things get done (notice the use of the passive voice, as if things *got done* on their own), and revise to edit out our tics and bad habits.

But coming up with a draft is always a challenge. And hearing critical feedback on something you've wrestled with can be even harder.

I was once having coffee with Sam, one of my grad students, a smart guy who describes himself as having "curious posture" and "British teeth" even though he's from the Midwest. We were going over his nearly complete—and excellent—final manuscript. I'd done a gentle copyedit, replacing some semicolons with periods and correcting typos.

After we'd settled in, I asked if he'd just learned the word *exacerbate* (to make worse). He'd used it when I knew he meant *exaggerate* (to make bigger).

Sam confessed that yes, he had recently learned the word; he liked it and wanted to put it in his thesis. As soon as he realized he'd messed up, he looked deep into his coffee cup and shook his head.

Then he got all serious and asked: "Is it normal to feel stupid after getting back an edited manuscript?"

Oh, my dear boy, I thought. *Welcome to my world.*

You feel stupid when someone points out mistakes from carelessness (*I knew that!*), and you feel stupid when someone shows you that you don't really know what a word you're using means (*exacerbate!*), and you feel stupid when it seems obvious to everyone in the room except you that you were writing around the hole in your donut. That feeling of stupidity can lead to shame.

What separates good writers from those who will never be better than mediocre is that good writers know they will often feel stupid or stuck, but they understand that doesn't mean they *are* stupid. They're stuck. And they learn to appreciate feedback. Sam knew my editing helped protect him. Criticism is like the sting of the vaccination needle. It hurts but is worth it in the long run.

If you worry about how your essay will be critiqued, if you think you might receive comments and suggestions that will hurt your feelings, or if you get conflicting advice and don't know whom to listen to, you're on the right track. That means that you care. Admitting what you don't know and asking for assistance is how you grow and learn.

The ideal time to start working on your application essays is the summer before senior year. By that point you should have a good idea of where you want to apply. The prompts will be available. Even if you have a super-busy summer (caddy camp; hiking in Nepal; reading all the books and essays I've recommended), you will have time to think, to come up with a list of topics, and to start writing.

Don't make the mistake of believing you need the right

> I went for years not finishing anything. Because, of course, when you finish something you can be judged.
>
> ERICA JONG

atmosphere, when the moon is in Capricorn and the wind is blowing at 7.3 miles per hour and the air smells like frangipani. If you wait until you feel like writing your application essay, you might be the oldest person ever to apply to college.

Writer's Block

You may get stuck. We all always get stuck. Being okay with stuckness is one of the traits successful writers share with scientists and anyone whose work is intellectually demanding. I don't believe in "writer's block." I don't believe in waiting for the muse to appear before you start to write. I don't believe in Santa or the Easter Bunny, either, though I'm always happy to have candy canes and Peeps.

Sometimes it helps to stop working for a while, to go for a walk or get another handful of Cheez-Its. But often you just have to tough it out. Put your butt in the chair and keep it there until you figure out what you need to do. It's uncomfortable, but often an essential part of the process.

When I'm really stuck or just plain miserable, I'll make a writing date with a friend. We'll go to a coffee shop, chat for a few minutes, and then open our laptops and get to work. Because writing can be so hard and lonely, it helps to have someone sitting across the table suffering with you. When I'm by myself, I tend to shift attention from what I'm supposed to be working on and might be tempted to check email. I'll *Like* every cute animal video on Facebook and, okay, if I'm being honest, shop for shoes. If another person sits tapping away at the keys, I feel too guilty to buy yet another pair of cowboy boots. These writing dates—whether they take place in a coffee shop, at the library, or in someone's house—can make work more fun.

When I come up with an idea, often it feels like a complete and beautiful thing. It lives in that perfect state until I start to write. Then all hell breaks loose. In the translation from my brain to the page, what seemed luminescent appears monstrous, or at best ungainly. I've learned to expect that and not to get too attached to my ideas before I start work.

If I'm writing something short, like an essay, I try to vomit out a complete draft in one sitting. I know it will be the thinking draft, the shitty first draft. I allow myself to suck and see what happens. I know I'll have to throw out many words to get to the right ones.

Sometimes, when I'm desperately, hopelessly stuck and have spent far too long staring at a blank page, I'll grab a book by a writer I love and copy out a sentence or a paragraph that I find exquisite. Maybe I'll type out a few lines of poetry from Wallace Stevens or a passage from an essay by Joan Didion. Sometimes I'll read aloud the giant sentence I quoted at the beginning of this book by Martin Luther King Jr. That exercise can serve both to inspire and to get me warmed up.

Many times I've had students read Tim O'Brien's *The Things They Carried* and then ask them to make a list of the things they carry, keeping in mind O'Brien's beautiful catalogs of what the soldiers in Vietnam kept with them, both material items and emotional baggage. My students come up with lists that are personal and unique and, yes, often beautiful. After an exercise like that, their writing tends to improve.

Find Your Readers

When I give feedback, I point out problems, but I also show students where they are totally hitting it. *YES!!!* I exclaim in the margin. It can be useful to have someone applaud the nice parts. Once I point out how well the student can write, I suggest ways to revise the rest of the essay to that level.

When you give your essay to someone else to read, ask them to mark your gold star sentence. If you give it to ten people, you might get ten different gold stars. That's great. Listen to each person's feedback. Ask yourself why they liked what they liked, and figure out how to clear up all their confusions and questions. There will likely be confusions and questions. Each time someone points out a problem, resist the urge to say, "Well, if you were smarter, you'd know what I meant." I sometimes have this reaction, and then mentally slap myself upside the head.

I know what you want when you give someone a draft. You want what most writers want. You hope people will read it and say, "There's a typo in the second paragraph, but other than that it's brilliant. It is the best essay I've ever read. Not only will this piece of gorgeous, honest, funny, insightful prose gain you admission to every college in the country and garner scholarships you haven't even applied for, it will be published in magazines and anthologized so that people all over the world can read it and be impressed."

Every time I give a draft to readers, some part of me wishes for that response. It has never happened. It will never happen. Each piece of work can benefit from someone else's critical eye. I love having editors who save me from myself.

We all need help. You get to decide how you respond to feedback. If I say a piece of writing has a problem, you can bet there's a problem. I may not be able to tell you how to fix it, or I may make a suggestion that shows what I would do and ask you to revise to sound like you. If someone says, "This seems flat," or "I don't believe you actually became best friends with that guy," or "I don't hear your voice in this," believe them and work to solve the problem.

It's hard and scary to show your work to someone, especially anyone whose opinion you value. But better to get help while you still can. You don't want your first reader to be someone who is in the position of evaluating you. Instead, give a draft of your essay to someone who loves you. A parent. A sibling. A friend. A teacher. But you have to train your readers to be more than cheerleaders. You'll have to tell them what you want from them; make sure to let them know you want serious feedback. People, like dogs, enjoy being useful and are often flattered to be asked for help.

And remind them to be gentle. I had many friends comment on drafts of this book and received heaps of useful suggestions. One reader's bossy tone, however, chafed. I had to remind myself that he was doing me a big fat favor and to be grateful for the help. When I comment on manuscripts, I try to ask questions instead of making demands. "Do you need a conclusion here?" stings less than "I want a concluding paragraph." It's not about what I want as a reader; it's about helping the writer accomplish what she is trying to do.

Value the time and effort of your helpers; don't give them a draft riddled with typos, spelling errors, and bad sentences. Readers like to feel smart, and it's easier to point out typos than it is to fully engage with the ideas, so get the draft as clean as you can make it, and then under-

> I love deadlines. I like the whooshing sound they make as they fly by.
>
> DOUGLAS ADAMS

stand that good feedback may force you into a new-blank-document revision. Your readers may pick out one sentence that seems like a throwaway to you but is actually the heart of the essay. That means you'll have to think about how to write a new draft around that bit.

Having people read your stuff is not cheating. It's a smart practice, something all writers do. Look at the acknowledgments section of just about any book, and you'll see how gratefully most authors thank the people who've helped them along the way. Just don't let anyone rewrite your sentences. You have to sound like you. Like the best, smartest version of you.

Remember, any writing or polishing you've done and thrown out is not a waste of time. It's helping you learn and getting you to where you need to go. The more you write, revise, and polish, the better writer you will become.

You Can Do This

You're worried. You're anxious. I don't blame you. This is an excruciating time of life.

You want to get this over with. Obsessing about the college application process may have taken over your every waking moment. You might believe (wrongly) that where you go to college will determine the course of the rest of your life. You want to write a perfect essay on the perfect topic, and you want it to be done now. It feels hard. It feels impossible.

Relax.

Breathe.

Remember to have fun.

You can do this.

ACKNOWLEDGMENTS

Most books are not like the Greek goddess of wisdom, Athena, who sprang fully grown from the head of her daddy, Zeus. No, friends, it takes a village to write a book, and this is where I get to thank the villagers.

Most important are the students I've worked with over the years who shared their fears, accomplishments, and funny stories with me—and allowed me to share them with you. I'm grateful to the following people who gave me permission to parade their foibles and allow me to brag about how spectacular they are: Jane Blicher, Lauren Buchholtz, Adam Fuhrman, Jamie Fuhrman, Tim Karu, Max Mankin, Peyton McGovern, Mark Pham, Daniel Ren, Emma Schlechter, Cecilia Scott, and "Amanda." Also my two undergraduate students Miranda Beckum and Breanna Howell.

As I've tried to make clear in the book, the most important part of writing is rewriting, and we all need readers who will point out places that aren't clear, tell you too many of your examples are about your dog, and keep you from making yet another reference to Taylor Swift. I've been fortunate to have an army of teen readers who have helped save me from myself. They are Michael Blicher, Simplicio (Tre) Deleon, Corey Edgar, Willa Fossum, Bailey Griffin, Abby Percy-Ratcliff, Daniel Ren, Braden Scherting, Emma Schlecter, Tara Stewart, and Claire Westerlund. The University of Chicago Press solicited reports from experts in college admissions and also from two undergrads, Olivia Cheng and Rachel Schonbaum, who gave me smart, critical readings.

A handful of grownup friends also gave it a rigorous read: David Brooks, Matthew Darjany, Martha Furst, Mark Haywood, Julie Mitchell, and Ruth Monnig. I'm grateful for conversations with admissions pros Julie McCulloh, Phil Ballinger, and especially Steve Handel, who was generous beyond what any author could reasonably expect. I learned so much from my former colleagues at Duke, particularly from Dean Christoph Guttentag.

After I wrote my first book about college admissions (which I now see as too snarky and full of the writing mistakes I've warned you about in this book), I thought I was done writing about the topic. And then Mary Laur, an editor at the University of Chicago Press, approached me with the idea for this project. We both wanted it to be about writing, not about the application process. We had so many weird things in common that it felt like kismet when we talked on the phone. As much as I complain about how hard it is to write, this one was actually a ton of fun to work on, largely because of Mary.

Part of the reason I was excited about publishing with the University of Chicago Press is because they have a long history of putting out excellent books about writing, including the *Chicago Manual of Style*. I knew I'd have a manuscript editor who would catch my mistakes and lucked out with Ruth Goring, who taught me a few new tricks in the process. I'm so grateful to the entire team at Chicago. They have made the hard work of writing a book less painful and at times even fun.

As a college professor, I have the best job in the world. I get to choose books (and essays) I love and talk about them with smart people. Much of what's in this book is the result of having taught wonderful creative writing students; I learn as much from them as they do from me. Many of my former students have become good friends. And friends of Helen. That dog loves students, and loves coming to class (where she often farts).

In the eleventh hour, Anastasia Hilton, Marci Riseman, and Caitlin Wheeler came through with speedy and expert proofreading. Anyone who finds a typo they missed wins a Snickers bar (or a beer, if legal). My debts to Valerie Chang just keep compounding. At this point, she owns me.